MznLnx

Missing Links Exam Preps

Exam Prep for

Integrated Arithmetic and Basic Algebra

Jordan, Palow, 3rd Edition

The MznLnx Exam Prep is your link from the texbook and lecture to your exams.
The MznLnx Exam Preps are unauthorized and comprehensive reviews of your textbooks.

All material provided by MznLnx and Rico Publications (c) 2010
Textbook publishers and textbook authors do not particpate in or contribute to these reviews.

MznLnx

Rico Publications

Exam Prep for Integrated Arithmetic and Basic Algebra
3rd Edition
Jordan, Palow

Publisher: Raymond Houge
Assistant Editor: Michael Rouger
Text and Cover Designer: Lisa Buckner
Marketing Manager: Sara Swagger
Project Manager, Editorial Production: Jerry Emerson
Art Director: Vernon Lowerui

Product Manager: Dave Mason
Editorial Assitant: Rachel Guzmanji
Pedagogy: Debra Long
Cover Image: Jim Reed/Getty Images
Text and Cover Printer: City Printing, Inc.
Compositor: Media Mix, Inc.

(c) 2010 Rico Publications
ALL RIGHTS RESERVED. No part of this work covered by the copyright may be reproduced or used in any form or by an means--graphic, electronic, or mechanical, including photocopying, recording, taping, Web distribution, information storage, and retrieval systems, or in any other manner--without the written permission of the publisher.

For more information about our products, contact us at:
Dave.Mason@RicoPublications.com

For permission to use material from this text or product, submit a request online to:
Dave.Mason@RicoPublications.com

Printed in the United States
ISBN:

Contents

CHAPTER 1
Basic Ideas — 1

CHAPTER 2
Adding and Subtracting Integers and Polynomials — 10

CHAPTER 3
Laws of Exponents, Products and Quotients of Integers and Polynomials — 23

CHAPTER 4
Linear Equations and Inequalities — 35

CHAPTER 5
Graphing Linear Equations and Inequalities — 49

CHAPTER 6
Systems of Linear Equations — 62

CHAPTER 7
Factors, Divisors, and Factoring — 71

CHAPTER 8
Multiplication and Division of Rational Numbers and Expressions — 80

CHAPTER 9
Addition and Subtraction of Rational Numbers and Expressions — 88

CHAPTER 10
Ratios, Percents, and Applications — 96

CHAPTER 11
Roots and Radicals — 100

CHAPTER 12
Solving Quadratic Equations — 106

ANSWER KEY — 110

TO THE STUDENT

COMPREHENSIVE

The *MznLnx* Exam Prep series is designed to help you pass your exams. Editors at MznLnx review your textbooks and then prepare these practice exams to help you master the textbook material. Unlike study guides, workbooks, and practice tests provided by the texbook publisher and textbook authors, *MznLnx* gives you **all** of the material in each chapter in exam form, not just samples, so you can be sure to nail your exam.

MECHANICAL

The MznLnx Exam Prep series creates exams that will help you learn the subject matter as well as test you on your understanding. Each question is designed to help you master the concept. Just working through the exams, you gain an understanding of the subject--its a simple mechanical process that produces success.

INTEGRATED STUDY GUIDE AND REVIEW

MznLnx is not just a set of exams designed to test you, its also a comprehensive review of the subject content. Each exam question is also a review of the concept, making sure that you will get the answer correct without having to go to other sources of material. You learn as you go! Its the easiest way to pass an exam.

HUMOR

Studying can be tedious and dry. MznLnx's instructional design includes moderate humor within the exam questions on occassion, to break the tedium and revitalize the brain

Chapter 1. Basic Ideas

1. A _____ is a symbol or group of symbols, or a word in a natural language that represents a number.
   a. Thing
   b. Numeral0
   c. Undefined
   d. Undefined

2. In mathematics, a _____ can mean either an element of the set {1, 2, 3, ...} (i.e the positive integers) or an element of the set {0, 1, 2, 3, ...} (i.e. the non-negative integers).
   a. Concept
   b. Whole number0
   c. Undefined
   d. Undefined

3. Mathematical _____ is used to represent ideas.
   a. Notation0
   b. Thing
   c. Undefined
   d. Undefined

4. The system of _____ numerals was a numeral system used in ancient Egypt. It was a decimal system, often rounded off to the higher power, written in hieroglyphs.
   a. Thing
   b. Egyptian0
   c. Undefined
   d. Undefined

5. _____ or arithmetics is the oldest and most elementary branch of mathematics, used by almost everyone, for tasks ranging from simple daily counting to advanced science and business calculations.
   a. Arithmetic0
   b. Thing
   c. Undefined
   d. Undefined

6. _____ numerals are a numeral system originating in ancient Rome, adapted from Etruscan numerals.
   a. Roman0
   b. Thing
   c. Undefined
   d. Undefined

7. In mathematics, a _____ is a countable collection of open covers of a topological space that satisfies certain separation axioms.
   a. Thing
   b. Development0
   c. Undefined
   d. Undefined

8. _____ is the mathematical action of repeatedly adding or subtracting one, usually to find out how many objects there are or to set aside a desired number of objects.
   a. Counting0
   b. Thing
   c. Undefined
   d. Undefined

9. _____ are objects, characters, or other concrete representations of ideas, concepts, or other abstractions.
   a. Thing
   b. Symbols0
   c. Undefined
   d. Undefined

10. _____ is a numeral system in which each position is related to the next by a constant multiplier, a common ratio, called the base or radix of that numeral system.
    a. Place value0
    b. Thing
    c. Undefined
    d. Undefined

Chapter 1. Basic Ideas

11. _____ is a kind of property which exists as magnitude or multitude. It is among the basic classes of things along with quality, substance, change, and relation.
    a. Thing
    b. Amount0
    c. Undefined
    d. Undefined

12. Compass and straightedge or ruler-and-compass _____ is the _____ of lengths or angles using only an idealized ruler and compass.
    a. Construction0
    b. Thing
    c. Undefined
    d. Undefined

13. Regrouping is the act of putting ones into groups of 10. For example, the 1 on the far right of 131 would be denoted _____ if the digit of the number being subtracted is larger than 1, such as 131-99.
    a. By 100
    b. Thing
    c. Undefined
    d. Undefined

14. The _____, the average in everyday English, which is also called the arithmetic _____ (and is distinguished from the geometric _____ or harmonic _____). The average is also called the sample _____. The expected value of a random variable, which is also called the population _____.
    a. Mean0
    b. Thing
    c. Undefined
    d. Undefined

15. The _____ of measurement are a globally standardized and modernized form of the metric system.
    a. Thing
    b. Units0
    c. Undefined
    d. Undefined

16. In business, particularly accounting, a _____ is the time intervals that the accounts, statement, payments, or other calculations cover.
    a. Period0
    b. Thing
    c. Undefined
    d. Undefined

17. In mathematics, the _____ inverse of a number x, denoted 1/x or x^{-1}, is the number which, when multiplied by x, yields 1. The _____ inverse of x is also called the reciprocal of x.
    a. Thing
    b. Multiplicative0
    c. Undefined
    d. Undefined

18. A _____ is the result of the addition of a set of numbers. The numbers may be natural numbers, complex numbers, matrices, or still more complicated objects. An infinite _____ is a subtle procedure known as a series.
    a. Sum0
    b. Thing
    c. Undefined
    d. Undefined

19. In mathematics, computing, linguistics, and related disciplines, an _____ is a finite list of well-defined instructions for accomplishing some task which, given an initial state, will terminate in a defined end-state.
    a. Concept
    b. Algorithm0
    c. Undefined
    d. Undefined

20. _____ is the act of putting ones into groups of 10.

Chapter 1. Basic Ideas

a. Regrouping0
b. Thing
c. Undefined
d. Undefined

21. In mathematics, a matrix can be thought of as each row or _____ being a vector. Hence, a space formed by row vectors or _____ vectors are said to be a row space or a _____ space.
a. Column0
b. Concept
c. Undefined
d. Undefined

22. In combinatorial mathematics, a _____ is an un-ordered collection of unique elements.
a. Concept
b. Combination0
c. Undefined
d. Undefined

23. In mathematics, _____ is an elementary arithmetic operation. When one of the numbers is a whole number, _____ is the repeated sum of the other number.
a. Thing
b. Multiplication0
c. Undefined
d. Undefined

24. An _____ or member of a set is an object that when collected together make up the set.
a. Thing
b. Element0
c. Undefined
d. Undefined

25. In mathematics, the _____ , or members of a set or more generally a class are all those objects which when collected together make up the set or class.
a. Elements0
b. Thing
c. Undefined
d. Undefined

26. A _____ is a symbolic representation denoting a quantity or expression. It often represents an "unknown" quantity that has the potential to change.
a. Variable0
b. Thing
c. Undefined
d. Undefined

27. An _____ is a number which is involved in addition. Numbers being added are considered to be the addends.
a. Addend0
b. Thing
c. Undefined
d. Undefined

28. In mathematics, an inequality is a statement about the relative size or order of two objects. For example 14 > 10, or 14 is _____ 10.
a. Greater than0
b. Thing
c. Undefined
d. Undefined

29. Mathematical _____ really refers to two distinct areas of research: the first is the application of the techniques of formal _____ to mathematics and mathematical reasoning, and the second, in the other direction, the application of mathematical techniques to the representation and analysis of formal _____.
a. Logic0
b. Thing
c. Undefined
d. Undefined

Chapter 1. Basic Ideas

30. In common philosophical language, a proposition or _____, is the content of an assertion, that is, it is true-or-false and defined by the meaning of a particular piece of language.
    a. Statement0
    b. Concept
    c. Undefined
    d. Undefined

31. A _____ is a negotiable instrument instructing a financial institution to pay a specific amount of a specific currency from a specific demand account held in the maker/depositor's name with that institution. Both the maker and payee may be natural persons or legal entities.
    a. Check0
    b. Thing
    c. Undefined
    d. Undefined

32. The plus and _____ signs are mathematical symbols used to represent the notions of positive and negative as well as the operations of addition and subtraction.
    a. Thing
    b. Minus0
    c. Undefined
    d. Undefined

33. _____ is a branch of mathematics concerning the study of structure, relation and quantity.
    a. Algebra0
    b. Concept
    c. Undefined
    d. Undefined

34. In Euclidean geometry, a _____ is the set of all points in a plane at a fixed distance, called the radius, from a given point, the center.
    a. Thing
    b. Circle0
    c. Undefined
    d. Undefined

35. _____ is a physical property of a system that underlies the common notions of hot and cold; something that is hotter has the greater _____.
    a. Thing
    b. Temperature0
    c. Undefined
    d. Undefined

36. A _____ is a method of using property as security for the payment of a debt.
    a. Thing
    b. Mortgage0
    c. Undefined
    d. Undefined

37. _____ is the fee paid on borrowed money.
    a. Thing
    b. Interest0
    c. Undefined
    d. Undefined

38. Multiple Signal Classification, also known as _____, is an algorithm used for frequency estimation and emitter location.
    a. Music0
    b. Thing
    c. Undefined
    d. Undefined

39. In mathematics, a _____ is the result of multiplying, or an expression that identifies factors to be multiplied.

Chapter 1. Basic Ideas

a. Product0
b. Thing
c. Undefined
d. Undefined

40. A _____ of a number is the product of that number with any integer.
   a. Thing
   b. Multiple0
   c. Undefined
   d. Undefined

41. In mathematics, factorization (British English: factorisation) or factoring is the decomposition of an object (for example, a number, a polynomial, or a matrix) into a product of other objects, or _____, which when multiplied together give the original.
   a. Thing
   b. Factors0
   c. Undefined
   d. Undefined

42. _____ is the ability to hold, receive or absorb, or a measure thereof, similar to the concept of volume.
   a. Capacity0
   b. Concept
   c. Undefined
   d. Undefined

43. In mathematics, a _____ number (or a _____) is a natural number that has exactly two (distinct) natural number divisors, which are 1 and the _____ number itself.
   a. Thing
   b. Prime0
   c. Undefined
   d. Undefined

44. _____ are activities that are governed by a set of rules or customs and often engaged in competitively.
   a. Thing
   b. Sports0
   c. Undefined
   d. Undefined

45. In mathematics, an _____, mean, or central tendency of a data set refers to a measure of the "middle" or "expected" value of the data set.
   a. Average0
   b. Concept
   c. Undefined
   d. Undefined

46. _____ the expected value of a random variable displays the average or central value of the variable. It is a summary value of the distribution of the variable.
   a. Thing
   b. Determining0
   c. Undefined
   d. Undefined

47. In mathematics, a _____ is the end result of a division problem. It can also be expressed as the number of times the divisor divides into the dividend.
   a. Thing
   b. Quotient0
   c. Undefined
   d. Undefined

48. _____ is a payment made by a company to its shareholders
   a. Thing
   b. Dividend0
   c. Undefined
   d. Undefined

Chapter 1. Basic Ideas

49. In mathematics, a _____ of an integer n, also called a factor of n, is an integer which evenly divides n without leaving a remainder.
   a. Divisor0
   b. Thing
   c. Undefined
   d. Undefined

50. A _____ is the part of the dividend that is left over when the dividend is not evenly divisible by the divisor.
   a. Thing
   b. Remainder0
   c. Undefined
   d. Undefined

51. The _____ is a theorem in mathematics which precisely expresses the outcome of the usual process of division of integers. The name is something of a misnomer, as it is a theorem, not an algorithm, i.e. a well-defined procedure for achieving a specific task — although the _____ can be used to find the greatest common divisor of two integers.
   a. Division Algorithm0
   b. Thing
   c. Undefined
   d. Undefined

52. _____ is a set, with some particular properties and usually some additional structure, such as the operations of addition or multiplication, for instance.
   a. Space0
   b. Thing
   c. Undefined
   d. Undefined

53. In plane geometry, a _____ is a polygon with four equal sides, four right angles, and parallel opposite sides. In algebra, the _____ of a number is that number multiplied by itself.
   a. Thing
   b. Square0
   c. Undefined
   d. Undefined

54. A _____ is 360° or 2δ radians.
   a. Turn0
   b. Thing
   c. Undefined
   d. Undefined

55. A _____ is a unit of length, usually used to measure distance, in a number of different systems, including Imperial units, United States customary units and Norwegian/Swedish mil. Its size can vary from system to system, but in each is between 1 and 10 kilometers. In contemporary English contexts _____ refers to either:
   a. Mile0
   b. Thing
   c. Undefined
   d. Undefined

56. U.S. liquid _____ is legally defined as 231 cubic inches, and is equal to 3.785411784 litres or abotu 0.13368 cubic feet. This is the most common definition of a _____. The U.S. fluid ounce is defined as 1/128 of a U.S. _____.
   a. Gallon0
   b. Thing
   c. Undefined
   d. Undefined

57. _____ is the property of a physical object that quantifies the amount of matter and energy it is equivalent to.
   a. Mass0
   b. Thing
   c. Undefined
   d. Undefined

58. Equivalence is the condition of being _____ or essentially equal.

| a. Thing | b. Equivalent0 |
| c. Undefined | d. Undefined |

59. A _____ is a numeral used to indicate a count. The most common use of the word today is to name the part of a fraction that tells the number or count of equal parts.
| a. Numerator0 | b. Thing |
| c. Undefined | d. Undefined |

60. A _____ is the part of a fraction that tells how many equal parts make up a whole, and which is used in the name of the fraction: "halves", "thirds", "fourths" or "quarters", "fifths" and so on.
| a. Concept | b. Denominator0 |
| c. Undefined | d. Undefined |

61. In mathematics, the additive inverse, or _____ of a number n is the number that, when added to n, yields zero. The additive inverse of n is denoted −n. For example, 7 is −7, because 7 + (−7) = 0, and the additive inverse of −0.3 is 0.3, because −0.3 + 0.3 = 0.
| a. Opposite0 | b. Thing |
| c. Undefined | d. Undefined |

62. In mathematics, the _____ of a number n is the number that, when added to n, yields zero. The _____ of n is denoted −n. For example, 7 is −7, because 7 + (−7) = 0, and the _____ of −0.3 is 0.3, because −0.3 + 0.3 = 0.
| a. Additive inverse0 | b. Thing |
| c. Undefined | d. Undefined |

63. In mathematics, the _____ of a number x, denoted 1/x or x^{-1}, is the number which, when multiplied by x, yields 1. The _____ of x is also called the reciprocal of x.
| a. Multiplicative inverse0 | b. Thing |
| c. Undefined | d. Undefined |

64. _____ element of an element x with respect to a binary operation * with identity element e is an element y such that x * y = y * x = e. In particular,
| a. Thing | b. Inverse0 |
| c. Undefined | d. Undefined |

65. In mathematics, a _____ or rhodonea curve is a sinusoid plotted in polar coordinates.
| a. Thing | b. Rose0 |
| c. Undefined | d. Undefined |

66. A _____ fraction is a fraction in which the absolute value of the numerator is less than the denominator--hence, the absolute value of the fraction is less than 1.
| a. Proper0 | b. Thing |
| c. Undefined | d. Undefined |

67. A _____ is a quantity that denotes the proportional amount or magnitude of one quantity relative to another.

8   Chapter 1. Basic Ideas

   a. Ratio0   b. Thing
   c. Undefined   d. Undefined

   68. The decimal separator is a symbol used to mark the boundary between the integral and the fractional parts of a decimal numeral. Terms implying the symbol used are _____ and decimal comma.
   a. Decimal point0   b. Concept
   c. Undefined   d. Undefined

   69. _____ is a mathematical science pertaining to the collection, analysis, interpretation or explanation, and presentation of data. It is applicable to a wide variety of academic disciplines, from the physical and social sciences to the humanities.
   a. Statistics0   b. Thing
   c. Undefined   d. Undefined

   70. In mathematics a _____ is a function which defines a distance between elements of a set.
   a. Metric0   b. Thing
   c. Undefined   d. Undefined

   71. The _____ is a decimalized system of measurement based on the metre and the gram.
   a. Concept   b. Metric system0
   c. Undefined   d. Undefined

   72. _____ is the process of reducing the number of significant digits in a number.
   a. Concept   b. Rounding0
   c. Undefined   d. Undefined

   73. A _____ signifies a point or points of probability on a subject e.g., the _____ of creativity, which allows for the formation of rule or norm or law by interpretation of the phenomena events that can be created.
   a. Principle0   b. Thing
   c. Undefined   d. Undefined

   74. In mathematics, defined and _____ are used to explain whether or not expressions have meaningful, sensible, and unambiguous values.
   a. Undefined0   b. Thing
   c. Undefined   d. Undefined

   75. In set theory and other branches of mathematics, the _____ of a collection of sets is the set that contains everything that belongs to any of the sets, but nothing else.
   a. Thing   b. Union0
   c. Undefined   d. Undefined

   76. In mathematics, the conjugate _____ or adjoint matrix of an m-by-n matrix A with complex entries is the n-by-m matrix A* obtained from A by taking the transpose and then taking the complex conjugate of each entry.
   a. Thing   b. Pairs0
   c. Undefined   d. Undefined

77. In arithmetic, _____ is a procedure for calculating the division of one integer, called the dividend, by another integer called the divisor, to produce a result called the quotient.
- a. Long division0
- b. Thing
- c. Undefined
- d. Undefined

78. In mathematics, a _____ function in the sense of algebraic geometry is an everywhere-defined, polynomial function on an algebraic variety V with values in the field K over which V is defined.
- a. Regular0
- b. Thing
- c. Undefined
- d. Undefined

79. In set theory and its applications throughout mathematics, _____ are a collection of sets (or sometimes other mathematical objects) that can be unambiguously defined by a property that all its members share.
- a. Classes0
- b. Thing
- c. Undefined
- d. Undefined

Chapter 2. Adding and Subtracting Integers and Polynomials

1. In mathematics, a _____ can mean either an element of the set {1, 2, 3, ...} (i.e the positive integers) or an element of the set {0, 1, 2, 3, ...} (i.e. the non-negative integers).
   a. Concept
   b. Whole number0
   c. Undefined
   d. Undefined

2. An _____ is a combination of numbers, operators, grouping symbols and/or free variables and bound variables arranged in a meaningful way which can be evaluated..
   a. Expression0
   b. Thing
   c. Undefined
   d. Undefined

3. A _____ is a symbolic representation denoting a quantity or expression. It often represents an "unknown" quantity that has the potential to change.
   a. Thing
   b. Variable0
   c. Undefined
   d. Undefined

4. In mathematics and the mathematical sciences, a _____ is a fixed, but possibly unspecified, value. This is in contrast to a variable, which is not fixed.
   a. Thing
   b. Constant0
   c. Undefined
   d. Undefined

5. A _____ is a symbol or group of symbols, or a word in a natural language that represents a number.
   a. Numeral0
   b. Thing
   c. Undefined
   d. Undefined

6. _____ is a mathematical operation, written a^n, involving two numbers, the base a and the exponent n.
   a. Thing
   b. Exponentiating0
   c. Undefined
   d. Undefined

7. _____ is a mathematical operation, written a^n, involving two numbers, the base a and the exponent n.
   a. Thing
   b. Exponentiation0
   c. Undefined
   d. Undefined

8. _____ has many meanings, most of which simply .
   a. Power0
   b. Thing
   c. Undefined
   d. Undefined

9. A _____ is a three-dimensional solid object bounded by six square faces, facets, or sides, with three meeting at each vertex.
   a. Cube0
   b. Thing
   c. Undefined
   d. Undefined

10. In mathematics, an inequality is a statement about the relative size or order of two objects. For example 14 > 10, or 14 is _____ 10.
    a. Greater than0
    b. Thing
    c. Undefined
    d. Undefined

Chapter 2. Adding and Subtracting Integers and Polynomials 11

11. In mathematics, _____ is an elementary arithmetic operation. When one of the numbers is a whole number, _____ is the repeated sum of the other number.
    a. Multiplication0
    b. Thing
    c. Undefined
    d. Undefined

12. _____, either of the curved-bracket punctuation marks that together make a set of _____
    a. Parentheses0
    b. Thing
    c. Undefined
    d. Undefined

13. In abstract algebra, _____ consists of sets with binary operations that satisfy certain axioms.
    a. Grouping0
    b. Thing
    c. Undefined
    d. Undefined

14. In financial mathematics, the _____ volatility of an option contract is the volatility _____ by the market price of the option based on an option pricing model.
    a. Implied0
    b. Thing
    c. Undefined
    d. Undefined

15. The _____ (symbol _____) and the millibar (symbol mbar, also mb) are units of pressure.
    a. Bar0
    b. Thing
    c. Undefined
    d. Undefined

16. In plane geometry, a _____ is a polygon with four equal sides, four right angles, and parallel opposite sides. In algebra, the _____ of a number is that number multiplied by itself.
    a. Square0
    b. Thing
    c. Undefined
    d. Undefined

17. The _____ are the only integral domain whose positive elements are well-ordered, and in which order is preserved by addition. Like the natural numbers, the _____ form a countably infinite set. The set of all _____ is usually denoted in mathematics by a boldface Z .
    a. Integers0
    b. Thing
    c. Undefined
    d. Undefined

18. In mathematics, a _____ is an expression that is constructed from one or more variables and constants, using only the operations of addition, subtraction, multiplication, and constant positive whole number exponents. is a _____. Note in particular that division by an expression containing a variable is not in general allowed in polynomials. [1]
    a. Polynomial0
    b. Thing
    c. Undefined
    d. Undefined

19. In arithmetic and algebra, when a number or expression is both preceded and followed by a binary operation, an _____ is required for which operation should be applied first.
    a. Thing
    b. Order of operations0
    c. Undefined
    d. Undefined

20. _____ is a kind of property which exists as magnitude or multitude. It is among the basic classes of things along with quality, substance, change, and relation.

Chapter 2. Adding and Subtracting Integers and Polynomials

    a. Thing
    c. Undefined
    b. Amount0
    d. Undefined

21. The _____ of measurement are a globally standardized and modernized form of the metric system.
    a. Units0
    c. Undefined
    b. Thing
    d. Undefined

22. The word _____ comes from the Latin word linearis, which means created by lines.
    a. Thing
    c. Undefined
    b. Linear0
    d. Undefined

23. _____ is the estimation of a physical quantity such as distance, energy, temperature, or time.
    a. Measurement0
    c. Undefined
    b. Thing
    d. Undefined

24. In mathematics a _____ is a function which defines a distance between elements of a set.
    a. Thing
    c. Undefined
    b. Metric0
    d. Undefined

25. The _____ is a decimalized system of measurement based on the metre and the gram.
    a. Metric system0
    c. Undefined
    b. Concept
    d. Undefined

26. A _____ is a function that assigns a number to subsets of a given set.
    a. Thing
    c. Undefined
    b. Measure0
    d. Undefined

27. A _____ is a unit of length, usually used to measure distance, in a number of different systems, including Imperial units, United States customary units and Norwegian/Swedish mil. Its size can vary from system to system, but in each is between 1 and 10 kilometers. In contemporary English contexts _____ refers to either:
    a. Mile0
    c. Undefined
    b. Thing
    d. Undefined

28. _____ is a concept in traditional logic referring to a "type of immediate inference in which from a given proposition another proposition is inferred which has as its subject the predicate of the original proposition and as its predicate the subject of the original proposition (the quality of the proposition being retained)."
    a. Conversion0
    c. Undefined
    b. Concept
    d. Undefined

29. In mathematics, factorization (British English: factorisation) or factoring is the decomposition of an object (for example, a number, a polynomial, or a matrix) into a product of other objects, or _____, which when multiplied together give the original.
    a. Thing
    c. Undefined
    b. Factors0
    d. Undefined

Chapter 2. Adding and Subtracting Integers and Polynomials 13

30. A _____ is a numeral used to indicate a count. The most common use of the word today is to name the part of a fraction that tells the number or count of equal parts.
   a. Numerator0
   b. Thing
   c. Undefined
   d. Undefined

31. A _____ is a quantity that denotes the proportional amount or magnitude of one quantity relative to another.
   a. Thing
   b. Ratio0
   c. Undefined
   d. Undefined

32. A _____ is the part of a fraction that tells how many equal parts make up a whole, and which is used in the name of the fraction: "halves", "thirds", "fourths" or "quarters", "fifths" and so on.
   a. Denominator0
   b. Concept
   c. Undefined
   d. Undefined

33. The decimal separator is a symbol used to mark the boundary between the integral and the fractional parts of a decimal numeral. Terms implying the symbol used are _____ and decimal comma.
   a. Concept
   b. Decimal point0
   c. Undefined
   d. Undefined

34. _____ is the distance around a given two-dimensional object. As a general rule, the _____ of a polygon can always be calculated by adding all the length of the sides together. So, the formula for triangles is P = a + b + c, where a, b and c stand for each side of it. For quadrilaterals the equation is P = a + b + c + d. For equilateral polygons, P = na, where n is the number of sides and a is the side length.
   a. Thing
   b. Perimeter0
   c. Undefined
   d. Undefined

35. The metre (or _____, see spelling differences) is a measure of length. It is the basic unit of length in the metric system and in the International System of Units (SI), used around the world for general and scientific purposes.
   a. Meter0
   b. Concept
   c. Undefined
   d. Undefined

36. A _____ is a unit of length in the metric system, equal to one thousand metres, the current SI base unit of length
   a. Kilometer0
   b. Thing
   c. Undefined
   d. Undefined

37. _____ is a set of numbers, in the broadest sense of the word, together with one or more operations, such as addition or multiplication.
   a. Thing
   b. Number system0
   c. Undefined
   d. Undefined

38. _____ is a numeral system in which each position is related to the next by a constant multiplier, a common ratio, called the base or radix of that numeral system.
   a. Thing
   b. Place value0
   c. Undefined
   d. Undefined

Chapter 2. Adding and Subtracting Integers and Polynomials

39. A _____ is the result of the addition of a set of numbers. The numbers may be natural numbers, complex numbers, matrices, or still more complicated objects. An infinite _____ is a subtle procedure known as a series.
- a. Sum0
- b. Thing
- c. Undefined
- d. Undefined

40. In geometry and trigonometry, a _____ is defined as an angle between two straight intersecting lines of ninety degrees, or one-quarter of a circle.
- a. Right angle0
- b. Thing
- c. Undefined
- d. Undefined

41. The _____ is the distance around a closed curve. _____ is a kind of perimeter.
- a. Thing
- b. Circumference0
- c. Undefined
- d. Undefined

42. In mathematics, a _____ is a two-dimensional manifold or surface that is perfectly flat.
- a. Thing
- b. Plane0
- c. Undefined
- d. Undefined

43. In Euclidean geometry, a _____ is the set of all points in a plane at a fixed distance, called the radius, from a given point, the center.
- a. Thing
- b. Circle0
- c. Undefined
- d. Undefined

44. The _____, the average in everyday English, which is also called the arithmetic _____ (and is distinguished from the geometric _____ or harmonic _____). The average is also called the sample _____. The expected value of a random variable, which is also called the population _____.
- a. Thing
- b. Mean0
- c. Undefined
- d. Undefined

45. In geometry, a _____ (Greek words diairo = divide and metro = measure) of a circle is any straight line segment that passes through the centre and whose endpoints are on the circular boundary, or, in more modern usage, the length of such a line segment. When using the word in the more modern sense, one speaks of the _____ rather than a _____, because all diameters of a circle have the same length. This length is twice the radius. The _____ of a circle is also the longest chord that the circle has.
- a. Thing
- b. Diameter0
- c. Undefined
- d. Undefined

46. In mathematics, _____ are essentially word problems that are designed to use mathematical critical thinking in everyday situations.
- a. Thing
- b. Application problems0
- c. Undefined
- d. Undefined

47. In finance, a _____ is collateral that the holder of a position in securities, options, or futures contracts has to deposit to cover the credit risk of his counterparty.

Chapter 2. Adding and Subtracting Integers and Polynomials 15

    a. Thing
    c. Undefined
    b. Margin0
    d. Undefined

48. In classical geometry, a _____ of a circle or sphere is any line segment from its center to its boundary. By extension, the _____ of a circle or sphere is the length of any such segment. The _____ is half the diameter. In science and engineering the term _____ of curvature is commonly used as a synonym for _____.
    a. Radius0
    c. Undefined
    b. Thing
    d. Undefined

49. In geometry, a _____ is defined as a quadrilateral where all four of its angles are right angles.
    a. Rectangle0
    c. Undefined
    b. Thing
    d. Undefined

50. A _____ is one of the basic shapes of geometry: a polygon with three vertices and three sides which are straight line segments.
    a. Triangle0
    c. Undefined
    b. Thing
    d. Undefined

51. _____ is electromagnetic radiation with a wavelength that is visible to the eye (visible _____) or, in a technical or scientific context, electromagnetic radiation of any wavelength.
    a. Light0
    c. Undefined
    b. Thing
    d. Undefined

52. Mathematical _____ is used to represent ideas.
    a. Notation0
    c. Undefined
    b. Thing
    d. Undefined

53. A _____ is a quadrilateral, which is defined as a shape with four sides, which has a pair of parallel sides.
    a. Thing
    c. Undefined
    b. Trapezoid0
    d. Undefined

54. A _____ is a four-sided plane figure that has two sets of opposite parallel sides.
    a. Parallelogram0
    c. Undefined
    b. Concept
    d. Undefined

55. In astronomy, geography, geometry and related sciences and contexts, a plane is said to be _____ at a given point if it is locally perpendicular to the gradient of the gravity field, i.e., with the direction of the gravitational force at that point.
    a. Thing
    c. Undefined
    b. Horizontal0
    d. Undefined

56. In mathematics, the additive inverse, or _____ of a number n is the number that, when added to n, yields zero. The additive inverse of n is denoted −n. For example, 7 is −7, because 7 + (−7) = 0, and the additive inverse of −0.3 is 0.3, because −0.3 + 0.3 = 0.
    a. Opposite0
    c. Undefined
    b. Thing
    d. Undefined

Chapter 2. Adding and Subtracting Integers and Polynomials

57. In mathematics, the _____ of a number n is the number that, when added to n, yields zero. The _____ of n is denoted −n. For example, 7 is −7, because 7 + (−7) = 0, and the _____ of −0.3 is 0.3, because −0.3 + 0.3 = 0.
    a. Thing
    b. Additive inverse0
    c. Undefined
    d. Undefined

58. In geometry, a _____ is a special kind of point, usually a corner of a polygon, polyhedron, or higher dimensional polytope. In the geometry of curves a _____ is a point of where the first derivative of curvature is zero. In graph theory, a _____ is the fundamental unit out of which graphs are formed
    a. Vertex0
    b. Thing
    c. Undefined
    d. Undefined

59. In geometry, two lines or planes if one falls on the other in such a way as to create congruent adjacent angles. The term may be used as a noun or adjective. Thus, referring to Figure 1, the line AB is the _____ to CD through the point B.
    a. Thing
    b. Perpendicular0
    c. Undefined
    d. Undefined

60. U.S. liquid _____ is legally defined as 231 cubic inches, and is equal to 3.785411784 litres or abotu 0.13368 cubic feet. This is the most common definition of a _____. The U.S. fluid ounce is defined as 1/128 of a U.S. _____.
    a. Thing
    b. Gallon0
    c. Undefined
    d. Undefined

61. In geometry, an _____ of a triangle is a straight line through a vertex and perpendicular to (i.e. forming a right angle with) the opposite side or an extension of the opposite side.
    a. Altitude0
    b. Concept
    c. Undefined
    d. Undefined

62. Transport or _____ is the movement of people and goods from one place to another.
    a. Transportation0
    b. Thing
    c. Undefined
    d. Undefined

63. The _____ of a solid object is the three-dimensional concept of how much space it occupies, often quantified numerically.
    a. Volume0
    b. Thing
    c. Undefined
    d. Undefined

64. _____ are of a number n in its third power-the result of multiplying it by itself three times.
    a. Thing
    b. Cubes0
    c. Undefined
    d. Undefined

65. In mathematics, _____ geometry was the traditional name for the geometry of three-dimensional Euclidean space — for practical purposes the kind of space we live in.
    a. Solid0
    b. Thing
    c. Undefined
    d. Undefined

Chapter 2. Adding and Subtracting Integers and Polynomials

66. In mathematics, a _____ is a quadric surface, with the following equation in Cartesian coordinates: $(x/a)^2 + (y/b)^2 = 1$.
    a. Cylinder0
    b. Thing
    c. Undefined
    d. Undefined

67. A _____ is a three-dimensional geometric shape formed by straight lines through a fixed point (vertex) to the points of a fixed curve (directrix)
    a. Concept
    b. Cone0
    c. Undefined
    d. Undefined

68. _____ are cubes in which all sides are of the same length and all face perpendicular to each other including an atom at each corner of the unigt cell.
    a. Thing
    b. Cubic units0
    c. Undefined
    d. Undefined

69. _____ is a set, with some particular properties and usually some additional structure, such as the operations of addition or multiplication, for instance.
    a. Thing
    b. Space0
    c. Undefined
    d. Undefined

70. In geometry, the _____ of an object is a point in some sense in the middle of the object.
    a. Center0
    b. Thing
    c. Undefined
    d. Undefined

71. _____ is the application of tools and a processing medium to the transformation of raw materials into finished goods for sale.
    a. Manufacturing0
    b. Thing
    c. Undefined
    d. Undefined

72. In mathematics, a _____ is the set of all points in three-dimensional space (R^3) which are at distance r from a fixed point of that space, where r is a positive real number called the radius of the _____. The fixed point is called the center or centre, and is not part of the _____ itself.
    a. Thing
    b. Sphere0
    c. Undefined
    d. Undefined

73. The act of _____ is the calculated approximation of a result which is usable even if input data may be incomplete, uncertain, or noisy.
    a. Estimating0
    b. Thing
    c. Undefined
    d. Undefined

74. An _____ or member of a set is an object that when collected together make up the set.
    a. Element0
    b. Thing
    c. Undefined
    d. Undefined

75. In mathematics, the _____ , or members of a set or more generally a class are all those objects which when collected together make up the set or class.

Chapter 2. Adding and Subtracting Integers and Polynomials

a. Thing
b. Elements0
c. Undefined
d. Undefined

76. In mathematics, a _____ can mean either an element of the set {1, 2, 3, ...} (i.e the positive integers or the counting numbers) or an element of the set {0, 1, 2, 3, ...} (i.e. the non-negative integers).
a. Thing
b. Natural number0
c. Undefined
d. Undefined

77. A _____ is a set whose members are members of another set or a set contained within another set.
a. Thing
b. Subset0
c. Undefined
d. Undefined

78. A _____ is a number that is less than zero.
a. Negative number0
b. Thing
c. Undefined
d. Undefined

79. Mathematical _____ are the wide variety of ways to capture an abstract mathematical concept or relationship.
a. Thing
b. Representations0
c. Undefined
d. Undefined

80. _____ is a physical property of a system that underlies the common notions of hot and cold; something that is hotter has the greater _____.
a. Thing
b. Temperature0
c. Undefined
d. Undefined

81. A _____ is a one-dimensional picture in which the integers are shown as specially-marked points evenly spaced on a line.
a. Thing
b. Number line0
c. Undefined
d. Undefined

82. _____, verti-bar, vertical line, divider line, or pipe is the name of the character .
a. Thing
b. Vertical bar0
c. Undefined
d. Undefined

83. In mathematics, the _____ (or modulus) of a real number is its numerical value without regard to its sign.
a. Thing
b. Absolute value0
c. Undefined
d. Undefined

84. _____ are objects, characters, or other concrete representations of ideas, concepts, or other abstractions.
a. Symbols0
b. Thing
c. Undefined
d. Undefined

85. In topology and related areas of mathematics a _____ or Moore-Smith sequence is a generalization of a sequence, intended to unify the various notions of limit and generalize them to arbitrary topological spaces.

Chapter 2. Adding and Subtracting Integers and Polynomials

   a. Net0
   b. Thing
   c. Undefined
   d. Undefined

86. In a mathematical proof or a syllogism, a _____ is a statement that is the logical consequence of preceding statements.
   a. Concept
   b. Conclusion0
   c. Undefined
   d. Undefined

87. An _____ is a number which is involved in addition. Numbers being added are considered to be the addends.
   a. Thing
   b. Addend0
   c. Undefined
   d. Undefined

88. In mathematics, _____ expressions is used to reduce the expression into the lowest possible term.
   a. Thing
   b. Simplifying0
   c. Undefined
   d. Undefined

89. The _____ is a property of multiplication or addition where the product or sum remains the same, regardless of whether or not the order of the addends or factors are changed.
   a. Commutative property0
   b. Thing
   c. Undefined
   d. Undefined

90. _____ element of an element x with respect to a binary operation * with identity element e is an element y such that $x * y = y * x = e$. In particular,
   a. Thing
   b. Inverse0
   c. Undefined
   d. Undefined

91. In mathematics, the _____ inverse, or opposite, of a number n is the number that, when added to n, yields zero. The _____ inverse of n is denoted −n.
   a. Additive0
   b. Thing
   c. Undefined
   d. Undefined

92. In mathematics, _____ is a property that a binary operation can have. Within an expression containing two or more of the same associative operators in a row, the order of operations does not matter as long as the sequence of the operands is not changed.
   a. Thing
   b. Associativity0
   c. Undefined
   d. Undefined

93. In mathematics, a _____ may be described informally as a number that can be given by an infinite decimal representation.
   a. Thing
   b. Real number0
   c. Undefined
   d. Undefined

94. An _____ is an equality that remains true regardless of the values of any variables that appear within it, to distinguish it from an equality which is true under more particular conditions.

Chapter 2. Adding and Subtracting Integers and Polynomials

a. Identity0
b. Thing
c. Undefined
d. Undefined

95. In mathematics the _____ of a set which is equipped with the operation of addition is an element which, when added to any other element x in the set, yields x.
   a. Concept
   b. Additive identity0
   c. Undefined
   d. Undefined

96. In mathematics, computing, linguistics, and related disciplines, an _____ is a finite list of well-defined instructions for accomplishing some task which, given an initial state, will terminate in a defined end-state.
   a. Algorithm0
   b. Concept
   c. Undefined
   d. Undefined

97. In banking and accountancy, the outstanding _____ is the amount of money owned, or due, that remains in a deposit account or a loan account at a given date, after all past remittances, payments and withdrawal have been accounted for.
   a. Thing
   b. Balance0
   c. Undefined
   d. Undefined

98. _____, also known as Omicron Ceti (or ï Ceti / ï Cet), is a red giant star approximately 418 light-years away in the constellation Cetus. _____ is a binary star, _____ A being the giant, along with _____ B.
   a. Mira0
   b. Thing
   c. Undefined
   d. Undefined

99. A _____ is a system of payment named after the small plastic card issued to users of the system.
   a. Thing
   b. Credit card0
   c. Undefined
   d. Undefined

100. In mathematics, a matrix can be thought of as each row or _____ being a vector. Hence, a space formed by row vectors or _____ vectors are said to be a row space or a _____ space.
   a. Concept
   b. Column0
   c. Undefined
   d. Undefined

101. In mathematics, a _____ is the result of multiplying, or an expression that identifies factors to be multiplied.
   a. Product0
   b. Thing
   c. Undefined
   d. Undefined

102. In mathematics, a _____ is the end result of a division problem. It can also be expressed as the number of times the divisor divides into the dividend.
   a. Thing
   b. Quotient0
   c. Undefined
   d. Undefined

103. In mathematics, and in particular in abstract algebra, the _____ is a property of binary operations that generalises the distributive law from elementary algebra.

Chapter 2. Adding and Subtracting Integers and Polynomials

a. Distributive property0
b. Thing
c. Undefined
d. Undefined

104. In mathematics, a _____ is a constant multiplicative factor of a certain object. The object can be such things as a variable, a vector, a function, etc. For example, the _____ of $9x^2$ is 9.
a. Thing
b. Coefficient0
c. Undefined
d. Undefined

105. The _____ of a geographic location is its height above a fixed reference point, often the mean sea level.
a. Elevation0
b. Thing
c. Undefined
d. Undefined

106. _____, from Latin meaning "to make progress", is defined in two different ways. Pure economic _____ is the increase in wealth that an investor has from making an investment, taking into consideration all costs associated with that investment including the opportunity cost of capital.
a. Thing
b. Profit0
c. Undefined
d. Undefined

107. _____ or arithmetics is the oldest and most elementary branch of mathematics, used by almost everyone, for tasks ranging from simple daily counting to advanced science and business calculations.
a. Arithmetic0
b. Thing
c. Undefined
d. Undefined

108. _____ is a branch of mathematics concerning the study of structure, relation and quantity.
a. Concept
b. Algebra0
c. Undefined
d. Undefined

109. In mathematics, a set is called _____ if there is a bijection between the set and some set of the form {1, 2, ..., n} where n is a natural number.
a. Finite0
b. Thing
c. Undefined
d. Undefined

110. In mathematics, a _____ of an integer n, also called a factor of n, is an integer which evenly divides n without leaving a remainder.
a. Divisor0
b. Thing
c. Undefined
d. Undefined

111. A _____ is a polynomial consisting of three terms; in other words, it is the sum of three monomials.
a. Trinomial0
b. Thing
c. Undefined
d. Undefined

112. In mathematics, a _____ is a particular kind of polynomial, having just one term.
a. Thing
b. Monomial0
c. Undefined
d. Undefined

Chapter 2. Adding and Subtracting Integers and Polynomials

113. In elementary algebra, a _____ is a polynomial with two terms: the sum of two monomials. It is the simplest kind of polynomial except for a monomial.
- a. Thing
- b. Binomial0
- c. Undefined
- d. Undefined

114. In mathematics, there are several meanings of _____ depending on the subject.
- a. Thing
- b. Degree0
- c. Undefined
- d. Undefined

115. The _____ is the sum of the exponents of the variables in the term.
- a. Thing
- b. Degree of a term0
- c. Undefined
- d. Undefined

116. The _____ is the maximum of the degrees of all terms in the polynomial.
- a. Thing
- b. Degree of a polynomial0
- c. Undefined
- d. Undefined

117. _____ is an adjective usually refering to being in the centre.
- a. Central0
- b. Thing
- c. Undefined
- d. Undefined

118. _____ is a business term for the amount of money that a company receives from its activities in a given period, mostly from sales of products and/or services to customers
- a. Thing
- b. Revenue0
- c. Undefined
- d. Undefined

119. A _____ is a negotiable instrument instructing a financial institution to pay a specific amount of a specific currency from a specific demand account held in the maker/depositor's name with that institution. Both the maker and payee may be natural persons or legal entities.
- a. Thing
- b. Check0
- c. Undefined
- d. Undefined

120. A _____ surface is the surface or face of a solid on its sides. It can also be defined as any face or surface that is not a base.
- a. Thing
- b. Lateral0
- c. Undefined
- d. Undefined

121. A _____ is a polygon with four sides and four vertices.
- a. Quadrilateral0
- b. Thing
- c. Undefined
- d. Undefined

122. In mathematics, a _____ is an n-tuple with n being 3.
- a. Triple0
- b. Thing
- c. Undefined
- d. Undefined

Chapter 3. Laws of Exponents, Products and Quotients of Integers and Polynomials

1. In mathematics, a _____ can mean either an element of the set {1, 2, 3, ...} (i.e the positive integers) or an element of the set {0, 1, 2, 3, ...} (i.e. the non-negative integers).
   - a. Concept
   - b. Whole number0
   - c. Undefined
   - d. Undefined

2. In mathematics, a _____ is the result of multiplying, or an expression that identifies factors to be multiplied.
   - a. Thing
   - b. Product0
   - c. Undefined
   - d. Undefined

3. In mathematics, _____ is an elementary arithmetic operation. When one of the numbers is a whole number, _____ is the repeated sum of the other number.
   - a. Multiplication0
   - b. Thing
   - c. Undefined
   - d. Undefined

4. _____ or arithmetics is the oldest and most elementary branch of mathematics, used by almost everyone, for tasks ranging from simple daily counting to advanced science and business calculations.
   - a. Thing
   - b. Arithmetic0
   - c. Undefined
   - d. Undefined

5. A _____ is a number that is less than zero.
   - a. Thing
   - b. Negative number0
   - c. Undefined
   - d. Undefined

6. The _____ is a property of multiplication or addition where the product or sum remains the same, regardless of whether or not the order of the addends or factors are changed.
   - a. Thing
   - b. Commutative property0
   - c. Undefined
   - d. Undefined

7. In mathematics, _____ is a property that a binary operation can have. Within an expression containing two or more of the same associative operators in a row, the order of operations does not matter as long as the sequence of the operands is not changed.
   - a. Thing
   - b. Associativity0
   - c. Undefined
   - d. Undefined

8. In mathematics, factorization (British English: factorisation) or factoring is the decomposition of an object (for example, a number, a polynomial, or a matrix) into a product of other objects, or _____, which when multiplied together give the original.
   - a. Factors0
   - b. Thing
   - c. Undefined
   - d. Undefined

9. _____ has many meanings, most of which simply .
   - a. Thing
   - b. Power0
   - c. Undefined
   - d. Undefined

10. _____, either of the curved-bracket punctuation marks that together make a set of _____

Chapter 3. Laws of Exponents, Products and Quotients of Integers and Polynomials

    a. Thing
    b. Parentheses0
    c. Undefined
    d. Undefined

11. In plane geometry, a _____ is a polygon with four equal sides, four right angles, and parallel opposite sides. In algebra, the _____ of a number is that number multiplied by itself.
    a. Thing
    b. Square0
    c. Undefined
    d. Undefined

12. In mathematics, the additive inverse, or _____ of a number n is the number that, when added to n, yields zero. The additive inverse of n is denoted −n. For example, 7 is −7, because 7 + (−7) = 0, and the additive inverse of −0.3 is 0.3, because −0.3 + 0.3 = 0.
    a. Thing
    b. Opposite0
    c. Undefined
    d. Undefined

13. In mathematics, the _____ of a number n is the number that, when added to n, yields zero. The _____ of n is denoted −n. For example, 7 is −7, because 7 + (−7) = 0, and the _____ of −0.3 is 0.3, because −0.3 + 0.3 = 0.
    a. Thing
    b. Additive inverse0
    c. Undefined
    d. Undefined

14. A _____ is a three-dimensional solid object bounded by six square faces, facets, or sides, with three meeting at each vertex.
    a. Thing
    b. Cube0
    c. Undefined
    d. Undefined

15. _____ is a way of expressing a number as a fraction of 100 per cent meaning "per hundred".
    a. Percent0
    b. Thing
    c. Undefined
    d. Undefined

16. The _____, the average in everyday English, which is also called the arithmetic _____ (and is distinguished from the geometric _____ or harmonic _____). The average is also called the sample _____. The expected value of a random variable, which is also called the population _____.
    a. Mean0
    b. Thing
    c. Undefined
    d. Undefined

17. In mathematics, a _____ is the end result of a division problem. It can also be expressed as the number of times the divisor divides into the dividend.
    a. Thing
    b. Quotient0
    c. Undefined
    d. Undefined

18. _____ is a mathematical operation, written a^n, involving two numbers, the base a and the exponent n.
    a. Thing
    b. Exponentiating0
    c. Undefined
    d. Undefined

19. _____ is a mathematical operation, written a^n, involving two numbers, the base a and the exponent n.

Chapter 3. Laws of Exponents, Products and Quotients of Integers and Polynomials

a. Exponentiation0
b. Thing
c. Undefined
d. Undefined

20. The _____ are the only integral domain whose positive elements are well-ordered, and in which order is preserved by addition. Like the natural numbers, the _____ form a countably infinite set. The set of all _____ is usually denoted in mathematics by a boldface Z.
    a. Integers0
    b. Thing
    c. Undefined
    d. Undefined

21. In mathematics, a _____ is an expression that is constructed from one or more variables and constants, using only the operations of addition, subtraction, multiplication, and constant positive whole number exponents. is a _____. Note in particular that division by an expression containing a variable is not in general allowed in polynomials. [1]
    a. Thing
    b. Polynomial0
    c. Undefined
    d. Undefined

22. _____ element of an element x with respect to a binary operation * with identity element e is an element y such that x * y = y * x = e. In particular,
    a. Thing
    b. Inverse0
    c. Undefined
    d. Undefined

23. _____ is a physical property of a system that underlies the common notions of hot and cold; something that is hotter has the greater _____.
    a. Temperature0
    b. Thing
    c. Undefined
    d. Undefined

24. A _____ is a landform that extends above the surrounding terrain in a limited area. A _____ is generally steeper than a hill, but there is no universally accepted standard definition for the height of a _____ or a hill although a _____ usually has an identifiable summit.
    a. Mountain0
    b. Thing
    c. Undefined
    d. Undefined

25. The _____ of a geographic location is its height above a fixed reference point, often the mean sea level.
    a. Thing
    b. Elevation0
    c. Undefined
    d. Undefined

26. A _____ is a special kind of ratio, indicating a relationship between two measurements with different units, such as miles to gallons or cents to pounds.
    a. Thing
    b. Rate0
    c. Undefined
    d. Undefined

27. In mathematics, an _____, mean, or central tendency of a data set refers to a measure of the "middle" or "expected" value of the data set.
    a. Concept
    b. Average0
    c. Undefined
    d. Undefined

28. In astronomy, geography, geometry and related sciences and contexts, a plane is said to be _____ at a given point if it is locally perpendicular to the gradient of the gravity field, i.e., with the direction of the gravitational force at that point.
   a. Thing
   b. Horizontal0
   c. Undefined
   d. Undefined

29. An _____ is an equality that remains true regardless of the values of any variables that appear within it, to distinguish it from an equality which is true under more particular conditions.
   a. Identity0
   b. Thing
   c. Undefined
   d. Undefined

30. In mathematics, a _____ or rhodonea curve is a sinusoid plotted in polar coordinates.
   a. Thing
   b. Rose0
   c. Undefined
   d. Undefined

31. In mathematics, and in particular in abstract algebra, the _____ is a property of binary operations that generalises the distributive law from elementary algebra.
   a. Distributive property0
   b. Thing
   c. Undefined
   d. Undefined

32. An _____ is a combination of numbers, operators, grouping symbols and/or free variables and bound variables arranged in a meaningful way which can be evaluated..
   a. Expression0
   b. Thing
   c. Undefined
   d. Undefined

33. In mathematics, a matrix can be thought of as each row or _____ being a vector. Hence, a space formed by row vectors or _____ vectors are said to be a row space or a _____ space.
   a. Concept
   b. Column0
   c. Undefined
   d. Undefined

34. In mathematics, _____ growth occurs when the growth rate of a function is always proportional to the function's current size.
   a. Thing
   b. Exponential0
   c. Undefined
   d. Undefined

35. In mathematics and the mathematical sciences, a _____ is a fixed, but possibly unspecified, value. This is in contrast to a variable, which is not fixed.
   a. Thing
   b. Constant0
   c. Undefined
   d. Undefined

36. A _____ is a symbolic representation denoting a quantity or expression. It often represents an "unknown" quantity that has the potential to change.
   a. Thing
   b. Variable0
   c. Undefined
   d. Undefined

37. In mathematics, a _____ is a constant multiplicative factor of a certain object. The object can be such things as a variable, a vector, a function, etc. For example, the _____ of $9x^2$ is 9.

Chapter 3. Laws of Exponents, Products and Quotients of Integers and Polynomials 27

    a. Thing
    b. Coefficient0
    c. Undefined
    d. Undefined

38. In mathematics, _____ expressions is used to reduce the expression into the lowest possible term.
    a. Thing
    b. Simplifying0
    c. Undefined
    d. Undefined

39. In elementary algebra, an _____ is a set that contains every real number between two indicated numbers and may contain the two numbers themselves.
    a. Thing
    b. Interval0
    c. Undefined
    d. Undefined

40. _____ are a measure of time.
    a. Minutes0
    b. Thing
    c. Undefined
    d. Undefined

41. In common philosophical language, a proposition or _____, is the content of an assertion, that is, it is true-or-false and defined by the meaning of a particular piece of language.
    a. Concept
    b. Statement0
    c. Undefined
    d. Undefined

42. A _____ is a negotiable instrument instructing a financial institution to pay a specific amount of a specific currency from a specific demand account held in the maker/depositor's name with that institution. Both the maker and payee may be natural persons or legal entities.
    a. Check0
    b. Thing
    c. Undefined
    d. Undefined

43. In geometry, the _____ of an object is a point in some sense in the middle of the object.
    a. Center0
    b. Thing
    c. Undefined
    d. Undefined

44. A _____ signifies a point or points of probability on a subject e.g., the _____ of creativity, which allows for the formation of rule or norm or law by interpretation of the phenomena events that can be created.
    a. Thing
    b. Principle0
    c. Undefined
    d. Undefined

45. The deductive-nomological model is a formalized view of scientific _____ in natural language.
    a. Thing
    b. Explanation0
    c. Undefined
    d. Undefined

46. In mathematics, a _____ is a particular kind of polynomial, having just one term.
    a. Monomial0
    b. Thing
    c. Undefined
    d. Undefined

47. In elementary algebra, a _____ is a polynomial with two terms: the sum of two monomials. It is the simplest kind of polynomial except for a monomial.

28   Chapter 3. Laws of Exponents, Products and Quotients of Integers and Polynomials

a. Binomial0   b. Thing
c. Undefined   d. Undefined

48. _____ is a numeral system in which each position is related to the next by a constant multiplier, a common ratio, called the base or radix of that numeral system.
a. Place value0   b. Thing
c. Undefined   d. Undefined

49. In geometry, a _____ is defined as a quadrilateral where all four of its angles are right angles.
a. Thing   b. Rectangle0
c. Undefined   d. Undefined

50. A _____ is one of the basic shapes of geometry: a polygon with three vertices and three sides which are straight line segments.
a. Triangle0   b. Thing
c. Undefined   d. Undefined

51. A _____ is a polynomial consisting of three terms; in other words, it is the sum of three monomials.
a. Thing   b. Trinomial0
c. Undefined   d. Undefined

52. _____ is the fee paid on borrowed money.
a. Interest0   b. Thing
c. Undefined   d. Undefined

53. A _____ is the result of the addition of a set of numbers. The numbers may be natural numbers, complex numbers, matrices, or still more complicated objects. An infinite _____ is a subtle procedure known as a series.
a. Sum0   b. Thing
c. Undefined   d. Undefined

54. In mathematics, the conjugate _____ or adjoint matrix of an m-by-n matrix A with complex entries is the n-by-m matrix A* obtained from A by taking the transpose and then taking the complex conjugate of each entry.
a. Thing   b. Pairs0
c. Undefined   d. Undefined

55. In algebra, a _____ is a binomial formed by taking the opposite of the second term of a binomial.
a. Thing   b. Conjugate0
c. Undefined   d. Undefined

56. In botany, _____ are above-ground plant organs specialized for photosynthesis. Their characteristics are typically analyzed by using Fiobonacci's sequences.
a. Leaves0   b. Thing
c. Undefined   d. Undefined

57. In mathematics the _____ refers to the identity: $a^2 - b^2 = (a+b)(a-b)$

Chapter 3. Laws of Exponents, Products and Quotients of Integers and Polynomials

a. Thing
b. Difference of two squares0
c. Undefined
d. Undefined

58. _____ are objects, characters, or other concrete representations of ideas, concepts, or other abstractions.
a. Thing
b. Symbols0
c. Undefined
d. Undefined

59. _____ are of a number n in its third power-the result of multiplying it by itself three times.
a. Thing
b. Cubes0
c. Undefined
d. Undefined

60. _____ is a set, with some particular properties and usually some additional structure, such as the operations of addition or multiplication, for instance.
a. Space0
b. Thing
c. Undefined
d. Undefined

61. In arithmetic and algebra, when a number or expression is both preceded and followed by a binary operation, an _____ is required for which operation should be applied first.
a. Thing
b. Order of operations0
c. Undefined
d. Undefined

62. In mathematics, defined and _____ are used to explain whether or not expressions have meaningful, sensible, and unambiguous values.
a. Thing
b. Undefined0
c. Undefined
d. Undefined

63. In mathematics, a _____ may be described informally as a number that can be given by an infinite decimal representation.
a. Real number0
b. Thing
c. Undefined
d. Undefined

64. A _____ is a numeral used to indicate a count. The most common use of the word today is to name the part of a fraction that tells the number or count of equal parts.
a. Numerator0
b. Thing
c. Undefined
d. Undefined

65. A _____ is the part of a fraction that tells how many equal parts make up a whole, and which is used in the name of the fraction: "halves", "thirds", "fourths" or "quarters", "fifths" and so on.
a. Concept
b. Denominator0
c. Undefined
d. Undefined

66. The _____ (symbol _____) and the millibar (symbol mbar, also mb) are units of pressure.
a. Thing
b. Bar0
c. Undefined
d. Undefined

67. In mathematics, the _____ (or modulus) of a real number is its numerical value without regard to its sign.

Chapter 3. Laws of Exponents, Products and Quotients of Integers and Polynomials

a. Absolute value0
b. Thing
c. Undefined
d. Undefined

68. A _____ fraction is a fraction in which the absolute value of the numerator is less than the denominator--hence, the absolute value of the fraction is less than 1.
    a. Proper0
    b. Thing
    c. Undefined
    d. Undefined

69. Acid _____ ratio measures the ability of a company to use its near cash or quick assets to immediately extinguish its current liabilities.
    a. Thing
    b. Test0
    c. Undefined
    d. Undefined

70. _____ the expected value of a random variable displays the average or central value of the variable.It is a summary value of the distribution of the variable.
    a. Determining0
    b. Thing
    c. Undefined
    d. Undefined

71. _____, from Latin meaning "to make progress", is defined in two different ways. Pure economic _____ is the increase in wealth that an investor has from making an investment, taking into consideration all costs associated with that investment including the opportunity cost of capital.
    a. Profit0
    b. Thing
    c. Undefined
    d. Undefined

72. The _____ is a method of finding the derivative of a function that is the quotient of two other functions for which derivatives exist.
    a. Quotient rule0
    b. Thing
    c. Undefined
    d. Undefined

73. _____ is a method for differentiating expressions involving exponentiation the power operation.
    a. Power rule0
    b. Thing
    c. Undefined
    d. Undefined

74. A _____ of a number is the product of that number with any integer.
    a. Multiple0
    b. Thing
    c. Undefined
    d. Undefined

75. _____ is a kind of property which exists as magnitude or multitude. It is among the basic classes of things along with quality, substance, change, and relation.
    a. Amount0
    b. Thing
    c. Undefined
    d. Undefined

76. In mathematics, a _____ is a statement that can be proved on the basis of explicitly stated or previously agreed assumptions.

Chapter 3. Laws of Exponents, Products and Quotients of Integers and Polynomials

a. Thing
c. Undefined
b. Theorem0
d. Undefined

77. A _____ is 360° or 2δ radians.
a. Thing
c. Undefined
b. Turn0
d. Undefined

78. Mathematical _____ is used to represent ideas.
a. Notation0
c. Undefined
b. Thing
d. Undefined

79. _____ is a notation for writing numbers that is often used by scientists and mathematicians to make it easier to write large and small numbers.
a. Scientific notation0
c. Undefined
b. Thing
d. Undefined

80. In economics _____ means before deductions brutto, e.g. _____ domestic or national product, or _____ profit or income
a. Thing
c. Undefined
b. Gross0
d. Undefined

81. The decimal separator is a symbol used to mark the boundary between the integral and the fractional parts of a decimal numeral. Terms implying the symbol used are _____ and decimal comma.
a. Concept
c. Undefined
b. Decimal point0
d. Undefined

82. A _____ is a one-dimensional picture in which the integers are shown as specially-marked points evenly spaced on a line.
a. Thing
c. Undefined
b. Number line0
d. Undefined

83. A _____ is a unit of length, usually used to measure distance, in a number of different systems, including Imperial units, United States customary units and Norwegian/Swedish mil. Its size can vary from system to system, but in each is between 1 and 10 kilometers. In contemporary English contexts _____ refers to either:
a. Mile0
c. Undefined
b. Thing
d. Undefined

84. _____ is the SI unit of energy.
a. Thing
c. Undefined
b. Joule0
d. Undefined

85. A _____ is a function that assigns a number to subsets of a given set.
a. Measure0
c. Undefined
b. Thing
d. Undefined

86. _____ is the property of a physical object that quantifies the amount of matter and energy it is equivalent to.

Chapter 3. Laws of Exponents, Products and Quotients of Integers and Polynomials

a. Thing
b. Mass0
c. Undefined
d. Undefined

87. In classical geometry, a _____ of a circle or sphere is any line segment from its center to its boundary. By extension, the _____ of a circle or sphere is the length of any such segment. The _____ is half the diameter. In science and engineering the term _____ of curvature is commonly used as a synonym for _____.
a. Thing
b. Radius0
c. Undefined
d. Undefined

88. In mathematics, _____ are essentially word problems that are designed to use mathematical critical thinking in everyday situations.
a. Thing
b. Application problems0
c. Undefined
d. Undefined

89. A _____ is a deliberate process for transforming one or more inputs into one or more results.
a. Calculation0
b. Thing
c. Undefined
d. Undefined

90. A _____ is a unit of length in the metric system, equal to one thousand metres, the current SI base unit of length
a. Thing
b. Kilometer0
c. Undefined
d. Undefined

91. The _____ is a unit of length nearly equal to the semi-major axis of Earth's orbit around the Sun. The currently accepted value of the AU is 149 597 870 691 ± 30 metres.
a. Astronomical unit0
b. Thing
c. Undefined
d. Undefined

92. An _____ or member of a set is an object that when collected together make up the set.
a. Element0
b. Thing
c. Undefined
d. Undefined

93. _____ is mass m per unit volume V.
a. Density0
b. Thing
c. Undefined
d. Undefined

94. The metre (or _____, see spelling differences) is a measure of length. It is the basic unit of length in the metric system and in the International System of Units (SI), used around the world for general and scientific purposes.
a. Concept
b. Meter0
c. Undefined
d. Undefined

95. A _____ given two distinct points A and B on the _____, is the set of points C on the line containing points A and B such that A is not strictly between C and B.
a. Ray0
b. Thing
c. Undefined
d. Undefined

Chapter 3. Laws of Exponents, Products and Quotients of Integers and Polynomials

96. The _____ in a vacuum is an important physical constant denoted by the letter c for constant or the Latin word celeritas meaning "swiftness
   a. Thing
   b. Speed of light0
   c. Undefined
   d. Undefined

97. _____ is electromagnetic radiation with a wavelength that is visible to the eye (visible _____) or, in a technical or scientific context, electromagnetic radiation of any wavelength.
   a. Light0
   b. Thing
   c. Undefined
   d. Undefined

98. The _____ or kilogramme is the SI base unit of mass. It is defined as being equal to the mass of the international prototype of the _____.
   a. Thing
   b. Kilogram0
   c. Undefined
   d. Undefined

99. In _____ algebra, a *-ring is an associative ring with an antilinear, antiautomorphism * : A ¨ A which is an involution.
   a. Star0
   b. Thing
   c. Undefined
   d. Undefined

100. _____ is the transport of people on a trip/journey or the process or time involved in a person or object moving from one location to another.
   a. Thing
   b. Travel0
   c. Undefined
   d. Undefined

101. In topology and related areas of mathematics a _____ or Moore-Smith sequence is a generalization of a sequence, intended to unify the various notions of limit and generalize them to arbitrary topological spaces.
   a. Thing
   b. Net0
   c. Undefined
   d. Undefined

102. _____ are economic entities that give rise to future economic benefit and is controlled by the entity as a result of past transaction or other events
   a. Asset0
   b. Thing
   c. Undefined
   d. Undefined

103. An _____ of a product of sums expresses it as a sum of products by using the fact that multiplication distributes over addition.
   a. Expansion0
   b. Thing
   c. Undefined
   d. Undefined

104. The word _____ comes from the Latin word linearis, which means created by lines.
   a. Thing
   b. Linear0
   c. Undefined
   d. Undefined

105. The _____ of a solid object is the three-dimensional concept of how much space it occupies, often quantified numerically.

Chapter 3. Laws of Exponents, Products and Quotients of Integers and Polynomials

a. Thing
b. Volume0
c. Undefined
d. Undefined

106. _____ is a unit of speed, expressing the number of international miles covered per hour.
a. Miles per hour0
b. Thing
c. Undefined
d. Undefined

107. The _____ governs the differentiation of products of differentiable functions.
a. Thing
b. Product rule0
c. Undefined
d. Undefined

108. A _____ is an equation in which each term is either a constant or the product of a constant times the first power of a variable.
a. Linear equation0
b. Thing
c. Undefined
d. Undefined

109. In mathematics, an _____ is a statement about the relative size or order of two objects.
a. Thing
b. Inequality0
c. Undefined
d. Undefined

Chapter 4. Linear Equations and Inequalities

1. The _____ are the only integral domain whose positive elements are well-ordered, and in which order is preserved by addition. Like the natural numbers, the _____ form a countably infinite set. The set of all _____ is usually denoted in mathematics by a boldface Z .
   - a. Integers0
   - b. Thing
   - c. Undefined
   - d. Undefined

2. In mathematics, and in particular in abstract algebra, the _____ is a property of binary operations that generalises the distributive law from elementary algebra.
   - a. Distributive property0
   - b. Thing
   - c. Undefined
   - d. Undefined

3. Two mathematical objects are equal if and only if they are precisely the same in every way. This defines a binary relation, _____, denoted by the sign of _____ "=" in such a way that the statement "x = y" means that x and y are equal.
   - a. Equality0
   - b. Thing
   - c. Undefined
   - d. Undefined

4. The word _____ comes from the Latin word linearis, which means created by lines.
   - a. Linear0
   - b. Thing
   - c. Undefined
   - d. Undefined

5. A _____ is an equation in which each term is either a constant or the product of a constant times the first power of a variable.
   - a. Linear equation0
   - b. Thing
   - c. Undefined
   - d. Undefined

6. An _____ is a combination of numbers, operators, grouping symbols and/or free variables and bound variables arranged in a meaningful way which can be evaluated..
   - a. Expression0
   - b. Thing
   - c. Undefined
   - d. Undefined

7. A _____ is a symbolic representation denoting a quantity or expression. It often represents an "unknown" quantity that has the potential to change.
   - a. Variable0
   - b. Thing
   - c. Undefined
   - d. Undefined

8. A _____ is a set of possible values that a variable can take on in order to satisfy a given set of conditions, which may include equations and inequalities.
   - a. Thing
   - b. Solution set0
   - c. Undefined
   - d. Undefined

9. Equivalence is the condition of being _____ or essentially equal.
   - a. Thing
   - b. Equivalent0
   - c. Undefined
   - d. Undefined

10. A _____ signifies a point or points of probability on a subject e.g., the _____ of creativity, which allows for the formation of rule or norm or law by interpretation of the phenomena events that can be created.

Chapter 4. Linear Equations and Inequalities

    a. Thing
    c. Undefined
    b. Principle0
    d. Undefined

11. In mathematics and the mathematical sciences, a _____ is a fixed, but possibly unspecified, value. This is in contrast to a variable, which is not fixed.
    a. Constant0
    b. Thing
    c. Undefined
    d. Undefined

12. In mathematics, _____ expressions is used to reduce the expression into the lowest possible term.
    a. Simplifying0
    b. Thing
    c. Undefined
    d. Undefined

13. In mathematics and more specifically set theory, the _____ set is the unique set which contains no elements.
    a. Empty0
    b. Thing
    c. Undefined
    d. Undefined

14. A _____ is a negotiable instrument instructing a financial institution to pay a specific amount of a specific currency from a specific demand account held in the maker/depositor's name with that institution. Both the maker and payee may be natural persons or legal entities.
    a. Check0
    b. Thing
    c. Undefined
    d. Undefined

15. _____ element of an element x with respect to a binary operation * with identity element e is an element y such that x * y = y * x = e. In particular,
    a. Inverse0
    b. Thing
    c. Undefined
    d. Undefined

16. In mathematics, the _____ inverse, or opposite, of a number n is the number that, when added to n, yields zero. The _____ inverse of n is denoted −n.
    a. Thing
    b. Additive0
    c. Undefined
    d. Undefined

17. In mathematics, the _____ of a number n is the number that, when added to n, yields zero. The _____ of n is denoted −n. For example, 7 is −7, because 7 + (−7) = 0, and the _____ of −0.3 is 0.3, because −0.3 + 0.3 = 0.
    a. Additive inverse0
    b. Thing
    c. Undefined
    d. Undefined

18. _____ forms part of thinking. Considered the most complex of all intellectual functions, _____ has been defined as higher-order cognitive process that requires the modulation and control of more routine or fundamental skills.
    a. Thing
    b. Problem solving0
    c. Undefined
    d. Undefined

19. A _____ is the result of the addition of a set of numbers. The numbers may be natural numbers, complex numbers, matrices, or still more complicated objects. An infinite _____ is a subtle procedure known as a series.

Chapter 4. Linear Equations and Inequalities

    a. Thing
    b. Sum0
    c. Undefined
    d. Undefined

20. _____ is a branch of mathematics concerning the study of structure, relation and quantity.
    a. Algebra0
    b. Concept
    c. Undefined
    d. Undefined

21. _____ over a given field is a polynomial with coefficients in that field.
    a. Thing
    b. Algebraic equation0
    c. Undefined
    d. Undefined

22. Acid _____ ratio measures the ability of a company to use its near cash or quick assets to immediately extinguish its current liabilities.
    a. Test0
    b. Thing
    c. Undefined
    d. Undefined

23. In mathematics, an _____ is a statement about the relative size or order of two objects.
    a. Inequality0
    b. Thing
    c. Undefined
    d. Undefined

24. The plus and _____ signs are mathematical symbols used to represent the notions of positive and negative as well as the operations of addition and subtraction.
    a. Minus0
    b. Thing
    c. Undefined
    d. Undefined

25. A _____ is a unit of length, usually used to measure distance, in a number of different systems, including Imperial units, United States customary units and Norwegian/Swedish mil. Its size can vary from system to system, but in each is between 1 and 10 kilometers. In contemporary English contexts _____ refers to either:
    a. Thing
    b. Mile0
    c. Undefined
    d. Undefined

26. _____ is a kind of property which exists as magnitude or multitude. It is among the basic classes of things along with quality, substance, change, and relation.
    a. Thing
    b. Amount0
    c. Undefined
    d. Undefined

27. _____ is a state in the southern region of the United States of America and was one of the original Thirteen Colonies that revolted against British rule in the American Revolution.
    a. Georgia0
    b. Thing
    c. Undefined
    d. Undefined

28. In chemistry, a _____ is substance made by combining two or more different materials in such a way that no chemical reaction occurs.
    a. Thing
    b. Mixture0
    c. Undefined
    d. Undefined

Chapter 4. Linear Equations and Inequalities

29. U.S. liquid _____ is legally defined as 231 cubic inches, and is equal to 3.785411784 litres or abotu 0.13368 cubic feet. This is the most common definition of a _____. The U.S. fluid ounce is defined as 1/128 of a U.S. _____.
   a. Gallon0
   b. Thing
   c. Undefined
   d. Undefined

30. In topology and related areas of mathematics a _____ or Moore-Smith sequence is a generalization of a sequence, intended to unify the various notions of limit and generalize them to arbitrary topological spaces.
   a. Thing
   b. Net0
   c. Undefined
   d. Undefined

31. According to the United Nations Statistics Division, _____ is the resale sale without transformation of new and used goods to retailers, to industrial, commercial, institutional or professional users, or to other wholesalers, or involves acting as an agent or broker in buying merchandise for, or selling merchandise, to such persons or companies.
   a. Wholesale0
   b. Thing
   c. Undefined
   d. Undefined

32. _____ is a term used in marketing to indicate how much the price of a product is above the cost of producing and distributing the product.
   a. Thing
   b. Markup0
   c. Undefined
   d. Undefined

33. A _____ is one of the basic shapes of geometry: a polygon with three vertices and three sides which are straight line segments.
   a. Triangle0
   b. Thing
   c. Undefined
   d. Undefined

34. _____ is the distance around a given two-dimensional object. As a general rule, the _____ of a polygon can always be calculated by adding all the length of the sides together. So, the formula for triangles is P = a + b + c, where a, b and c stand for each side of it. For quadrilaterals the equation is P = a + b + c + d. For equilateral polygons, P = na, where n is the number of sides and a is the side length.
   a. Perimeter0
   b. Thing
   c. Undefined
   d. Undefined

35. In mathematics, _____ are essentially word problems that are designed to use mathematical critical thinking in everyday situations.
   a. Thing
   b. Application problems0
   c. Undefined
   d. Undefined

36. In mathematics, _____ is an elementary arithmetic operation. When one of the numbers is a whole number, _____ is the repeated sum of the other number.
   a. Thing
   b. Multiplication0
   c. Undefined
   d. Undefined

37. _____ or arithmetics is the oldest and most elementary branch of mathematics, used by almost everyone, for tasks ranging from simple daily counting to advanced science and business calculations.

Chapter 4. Linear Equations and Inequalities

    a. Arithmetic0
    c. Undefined
    b. Thing
    d. Undefined

38. In mathematics, the _____ inverse of a number x, denoted 1/x or x^{-1}, is the number which, when multiplied by x, yields 1. The _____ inverse of x is also called the reciprocal of x.
    a. Thing
    c. Undefined
    b. Multiplicative0
    d. Undefined

39. In mathematics, a _____ is the result of multiplying, or an expression that identifies factors to be multiplied.
    a. Thing
    c. Undefined
    b. Product0
    d. Undefined

40. In mathematics, the multiplicative inverse of a number x, denoted 1/x or x^{-1}, is the number which, when multiplied by x, yields 1. The multiplicative inverse of x is also called the _____ of x.
    a. Thing
    c. Undefined
    b. Reciprocal0
    d. Undefined

41. In Euclidean geometry, a _____ is moving every point a constant distance in a specified direction.
    a. Concept
    c. Undefined
    b. Translation0
    d. Undefined

42. In mathematics, a _____ is the end result of a division problem. It can also be expressed as the number of times the divisor divides into the dividend.
    a. Thing
    c. Undefined
    b. Quotient0
    d. Undefined

43. The _____, the average in everyday English, which is also called the arithmetic _____ (and is distinguished from the geometric _____ or harmonic _____). The average is also called the sample _____. The expected value of a random variable, which is also called the population _____.
    a. Thing
    c. Undefined
    b. Mean0
    d. Undefined

44. _____ is a way of expressing a number as a fraction of 100 per cent meaning "per hundred".
    a. Thing
    c. Undefined
    b. Percent0
    d. Undefined

45. A _____ is a compensation which workers receive in exchange for their labor.
    a. Wage0
    c. Undefined
    b. Thing
    d. Undefined

46. A _____ is a special kind of ratio, indicating a relationship between two measurements with different units, such as miles to gallons or cents to pounds.
    a. Thing
    c. Undefined
    b. Rate0
    d. Undefined

Chapter 4. Linear Equations and Inequalities

47. The payment of _____ as remuneration for services rendered or products sold is a common way to reward sales people.
    a. Commission0
    b. Thing
    c. Undefined
    d. Undefined

48. _____ is the fee paid on borrowed money.
    a. Thing
    b. Interest0
    c. Undefined
    d. Undefined

49. A _____ are accounts maintained by commercial banks, savings and loan associations, credit unions, and mutual savings banks that pay interest but can not be used directly as money by, for example, writing a cheque.
    a. Savings account0
    b. Thing
    c. Undefined
    d. Undefined

50. In plane geometry, a _____ is a polygon with four equal sides, four right angles, and parallel opposite sides. In algebra, the _____ of a number is that number multiplied by itself.
    a. Square0
    b. Thing
    c. Undefined
    d. Undefined

51. _____ is a unit of speed, expressing the number of international miles covered per hour.
    a. Thing
    b. Miles per hour0
    c. Undefined
    d. Undefined

52. In statistics, _____ means the most frequent value assumed by a random variable, or occurring in a sampling of a random variable.
    a. Concept
    b. Mode0
    c. Undefined
    d. Undefined

53. In finance and economics, _____ is the process of finding the present value of an amount of cash at some future date, and along with compounding cash forms the basis of time value of money calculations.
    a. Thing
    b. Discount0
    c. Undefined
    d. Undefined

54. _____ is a fixed, but possibly unspecified, value. This is in contrast to a variable, which is not fixed.
    a. Thing
    b. Constant term0
    c. Undefined
    d. Undefined

55. In mathematics, a _____ is a constant multiplicative factor of a certain object. The object can be such things as a variable, a vector, a function, etc. For example, the _____ of $9x^2$ is 9.
    a. Thing
    b. Coefficient0
    c. Undefined
    d. Undefined

56. An _____ is an equality that remains true regardless of the values of any variables that appear within it, to distinguish it from an equality which is true under more particular conditions.

Chapter 4. Linear Equations and Inequalities

   a. Thing
   c. Undefined
   b. Identity0
   d. Undefined

57. _____ the expected value of a random variable displays the average or central value of the variable. It is a summary value of the distribution of the variable.
   a. Thing
   c. Undefined
   b. Determining0
   d. Undefined

58. In mathematics, a _____ may be described informally as a number that can be given by an infinite decimal representation.
   a. Thing
   c. Undefined
   b. Real number0
   d. Undefined

59. In common philosophical language, a proposition or _____, is the content of an assertion, that is, it is true-or-false and defined by the meaning of a particular piece of language.
   a. Statement0
   c. Undefined
   b. Concept
   d. Undefined

60. An _____ or member of a set is an object that when collected together make up the set.
   a. Thing
   c. Undefined
   b. Element0
   d. Undefined

61. In mathematics, the _____, or members of a set or more generally a class are all those objects which when collected together make up the set or class.
   a. Thing
   c. Undefined
   b. Elements0
   d. Undefined

62. A _____ is a fee added to a customer's bill.
   a. Thing
   c. Undefined
   b. Service charge0
   d. Undefined

63. _____ are activities that are governed by a set of rules or customs and often engaged in competitively.
   a. Thing
   c. Undefined
   b. Sports0
   d. Undefined

64. _____ are a measure of time.
   a. Thing
   c. Undefined
   b. Minutes0
   d. Undefined

65. In mathematics, _____ geometry was the traditional name for the geometry of three-dimensional Euclidean space — for practical purposes the kind of space we live in.
   a. Solid0
   c. Undefined
   b. Thing
   d. Undefined

66. In arithmetic and algebra, when a number or expression is both preceded and followed by a binary operation, an _____ is required for which operation should be applied first.

a. Thing
b. Order of operations0
c. Undefined
d. Undefined

67. In Euclidean geometry, a _____ is the set of all points in a plane at a fixed distance, called the radius, from a given point, the center.
a. Circle0
b. Thing
c. Undefined
d. Undefined

68. The _____ is the distance around a closed curve. _____ is a kind of perimeter.
a. Circumference0
b. Thing
c. Undefined
d. Undefined

69. In geometry, a _____ is defined as a quadrilateral where all four of its angles are right angles.
a. Rectangle0
b. Thing
c. Undefined
d. Undefined

70. The metre (or _____, see spelling differences) is a measure of length. It is the basic unit of length in the metric system and in the International System of Units (SI), used around the world for general and scientific purposes.
a. Concept
b. Meter0
c. Undefined
d. Undefined

71. A _____ is a quadrilateral, which is defined as a shape with four sides, which has a pair of parallel sides.
a. Thing
b. Trapezoid0
c. Undefined
d. Undefined

72. The _____ of a solid object is the three-dimensional concept of how much space it occupies, often quantified numerically.
a. Volume0
b. Thing
c. Undefined
d. Undefined

73. In mathematics, a _____ is a quadric surface, with the following equation in Cartesian coordinates: $(x/_a)^2 + (y/_b)^2 = 1$.
a. Thing
b. Cylinder0
c. Undefined
d. Undefined

74. A _____ is a unit of length in the metric system, equal to one thousand metres, the current SI base unit of length
a. Thing
b. Kilometer0
c. Undefined
d. Undefined

75. _____, Greek for "knowledge of nature," is the branch of science concerned with the discovery and characterization of universal laws which govern matter, energy, space, and time.
a. Thing
b. Physics0
c. Undefined
d. Undefined

76. _____ has many meanings, most of which simply .

Chapter 4. Linear Equations and Inequalities

   a. Thing
   c. Undefined
   b. Power0
   d. Undefined

77. A _____ is a one-dimensional picture in which the integers are shown as specially-marked points evenly spaced on a line.
   a. Number line0
   c. Undefined
   b. Thing
   d. Undefined

78. Mathematical _____ is used to represent ideas.
   a. Notation0
   c. Undefined
   b. Thing
   d. Undefined

79. In mathematics, an inequality is a statement about the relative size or order of two objects. For example 14 > 10, or 14 is _____ 10.
   a. Greater than0
   c. Undefined
   b. Thing
   d. Undefined

80. _____ interest refers to the fact that whenever interest is calculated, it is based not only on the original principal, but also on any unpaid interest that has been added to the principal.
   a. Thing
   c. Undefined
   b. Compound0
   d. Undefined

81. A _____ of a number is the product of that number with any integer.
   a. Multiple0
   c. Undefined
   b. Thing
   d. Undefined

82. A _____ is a number that is less than zero.
   a. Negative number0
   c. Undefined
   b. Thing
   d. Undefined

83. _____ are objects, characters, or other concrete representations of ideas, concepts, or other abstractions.
   a. Thing
   c. Undefined
   b. Symbols0
   d. Undefined

84. _____ means in succession or back-to-back
   a. Thing
   c. Undefined
   b. Consecutive0
   d. Undefined

85. _____, either of the curved-bracket punctuation marks that together make a set of _____
   a. Parentheses0
   c. Undefined
   b. Thing
   d. Undefined

86. In mathematics, a _____ function in the sense of algebraic geometry is an everywhere-defined, polynomial function on an algebraic variety V with values in the field K over which V is defined.

Chapter 4. Linear Equations and Inequalities

a. Thing
b. Regular0
c. Undefined
d. Undefined

87. In mathematics, a matrix can be thought of as each row or _____ being a vector. Hence, a space formed by row vectors or _____ vectors are said to be a row space or a _____ space.
a. Column0
b. Concept
c. Undefined
d. Undefined

88. In mathematics, an _____, mean, or central tendency of a data set refers to a measure of the "middle" or "expected" value of the data set.
a. Average0
b. Concept
c. Undefined
d. Undefined

89. In botany, _____ are above-ground plant organs specialized for photosynthesis. Their characteristics are typically analyzed by using Fiobonacci's sequences.
a. Thing
b. Leaves0
c. Undefined
d. Undefined

90. _____ is the transport of people on a trip/journey or the process or time involved in a person or object moving from one location to another.
a. Thing
b. Travel0
c. Undefined
d. Undefined

91. _____ is the largest city in the state of Texas and the fourth-largest in the United States. As of the 2005 U.S. Census estimate, it had a population of more than 2 million.
a. Houston0
b. Thing
c. Undefined
d. Undefined

92. _____ is a state located in the southern and southwestern regions of the United States of America.
a. Texas0
b. Thing
c. Undefined
d. Undefined

93. In sociology and biology a _____ is the collection of people or organisms of a particular species living in a given geographic area or space, usually measured by a census.
a. Thing
b. Population0
c. Undefined
d. Undefined

94. In probability theory, _____ are various sets of outcomes (a subset of the sample space) to which a probability is assigned.
a. Events0
b. Thing
c. Undefined
d. Undefined

95. In Euclidean geometry, a uniform _____ is a linear transformation that enlargers or diminishes objects, and whose _____ factor is the same in all directions. This is also called homothethy.

Chapter 4. Linear Equations and Inequalities

    a. Thing
    b. Scale0
    c. Undefined
    d. Undefined

96. A _____ is a landform that extends above the surrounding terrain in a limited area. A _____ is generally steeper than a hill, but there is no universally accepted standard definition for the height of a _____ or a hill although a _____ usually has an identifiable summit.
    a. Mountain0
    b. Thing
    c. Undefined
    d. Undefined

97. _____ is a form of periodic payment from an employer to an employee, which is specified in an employment contract.
    a. Thing
    b. Gross pay0
    c. Undefined
    d. Undefined

98. A _____ is a form of periodic payment from an employer to an employee, which is specified in an employment contract.
    a. Salary0
    b. Thing
    c. Undefined
    d. Undefined

99. The State of _____ is a state located in the Rocky Mountain region of the United States of America.
    a. Thing
    b. Colorado0
    c. Undefined
    d. Undefined

100. _____ are flexible, elastic objects used to store mechanical energy.
    a. Thing
    b. Springs0
    c. Undefined
    d. Undefined

101. _____ or investing is a term with several closely-related meanings in business management, finance and economics, related to saving or deferring consumption.
    a. Thing
    b. Investment0
    c. Undefined
    d. Undefined

102. A _____ is the part of the dividend that is left over when the dividend is not evenly divisible by the divisor.
    a. Thing
    b. Remainder0
    c. Undefined
    d. Undefined

103. The _____ of measurement are a globally standardized and modernized form of the metric system.
    a. Thing
    b. Units0
    c. Undefined
    d. Undefined

104. An _____ is the fee paid on borrow money.
    a. Interest rate0
    b. Concept
    c. Undefined
    d. Undefined

105. A _____ is a form of collective investment that pools money from many investors and invests their money in stocks, bonds, short-term money market instruments, and/or other securities.

a. Mutual fund0
b. Thing
c. Undefined
d. Undefined

106. _____ finance, in finance, a debt security, issued by Issuer
   a. Bond0
   b. Thing
   c. Undefined
   d. Undefined

107. _____ is electromagnetic radiation with a wavelength that is visible to the eye (visible _____) or, in a technical or scientific context, electromagnetic radiation of any wavelength.
   a. Light0
   b. Thing
   c. Undefined
   d. Undefined

108. In business, _____, _____ cost or _____ expense refers to an ongoing expense of operating a business.
   a. Overhead0
   b. Thing
   c. Undefined
   d. Undefined

109. In mathematics, a _____ or rhodonea curve is a sinusoid plotted in polar coordinates.
   a. Rose0
   b. Thing
   c. Undefined
   d. Undefined

110. _____ usually refers to money in the form of liquid currency, such as banknotes or coins.
   a. Thing
   b. Cash0
   c. Undefined
   d. Undefined

111. In set theory and other branches of mathematics, the _____ of a collection of sets is the set that contains everything that belongs to any of the sets, but nothing else.
   a. Union0
   b. Thing
   c. Undefined
   d. Undefined

112. The _____ is a popular form of gambling which involves the drawing of lots for a prize. Some governments forbid it, while others endorse it to the extent of organizign a national _____
   a. Thing
   b. Lottery0
   c. Undefined
   d. Undefined

113. Regrouping is the act of putting ones into groups of 10. For example, the 1 on the far right of 131 would be denoted _____ if the digit of the number being subtracted is larger than 1, such as 131-99.
   a. By 100
   b. Thing
   c. Undefined
   d. Undefined

114. A _____ is a function that assigns a number to subsets of a given set.
   a. Measure0
   b. Thing
   c. Undefined
   d. Undefined

115. In mathematics, there are several meanings of _____ depending on the subject.

a. Thing
b. Degree0
c. Undefined
d. Undefined

116. A pair of angles is _____ if their respective measures sum to 180 degrees.
   a. Concept
   b. Supplementary0
   c. Undefined
   d. Undefined

117. A pair of angles are _____ if the sum of their angles is 90°.
   a. Concept
   b. Complementary0
   c. Undefined
   d. Undefined

118. The existence and properties of _____ are the basis of Euclid's parallel postulate. _____ are two lines on the same plane that do not intersect even assuming that lines extend to infinity in either direction.
   a. Thing
   b. Parallel lines0
   c. Undefined
   d. Undefined

119. In mathematics, a _____ is a two-dimensional manifold or surface that is perfectly flat.
   a. Thing
   b. Plane0
   c. Undefined
   d. Undefined

120. In combinatorial mathematics, given a collection C of disjoint sets, a _____ is a set containing exactly one element from each member of the collection: it is a section of the quotient map induced by the collection.
   a. Thing
   b. Transversal0
   c. Undefined
   d. Undefined

121. In geometry, _____ lines are two lines that share one or more common points.
   a. Intersecting0
   b. Thing
   c. Undefined
   d. Undefined

122. In mathematics, the conjugate _____ or adjoint matrix of an m-by-n matrix A with complex entries is the n-by-m matrix A* obtained from A by taking the transpose and then taking the complex conjugate of each entry.
   a. Pairs0
   b. Thing
   c. Undefined
   d. Undefined

123. An _____ is an angle formed by two sides of a simple polygon that share an endpoint, namely, the angle on the inner side of the polygon.
   a. Interior angle0
   b. Thing
   c. Undefined
   d. Undefined

124. In set theory and other branches of mathematics, two kinds of complements are defined, the relative _____ and the absolute _____.
   a. Thing
   b. Complement0
   c. Undefined
   d. Undefined

125. In logic, a _____ consists of a logical incompatibility between two or more propositions.

a. Contradictions0
b. Thing
c. Undefined
d. Undefined

126. In geometry, two sets are called _____ if one can be transformed into the other by an isometry, i.e., a combination of translations, rotations and reflections.
   a. Thing
   b. Congruent0
   c. Undefined
   d. Undefined

127. _____ is the level of functional and/or metabolic efficiency of an organism at both the micro level.
   a. Health0
   b. Thing
   c. Undefined
   d. Undefined

128. _____ is an adjective usually refering to being in the centre.
   a. Central0
   b. Thing
   c. Undefined
   d. Undefined

129. In mathematics, a _____ can mean either an element of the set {1, 2, 3, ...} (i.e the positive integers) or an element of the set {0, 1, 2, 3, ...} (i.e. the non-negative integers).
   a. Concept
   b. Whole number0
   c. Undefined
   d. Undefined

Chapter 5. Graphing Linear Equations and Inequalities

1. The _____ are the only integral domain whose positive elements are well-ordered, and in which order is preserved by addition. Like the natural numbers, the _____ form a countably infinite set. The set of all _____ is usually denoted in mathematics by a boldface Z .
   a. Integers0
   b. Thing
   c. Undefined
   d. Undefined

2. _____ are the basic objects of study in graph theory. Informally speaking, a graph is a set of objects called points, nodes, or vertices connected by links called lines or edges.
   a. Thing
   b. Graphs0
   c. Undefined
   d. Undefined

3. The _____ (symbol _____) and the millibar (symbol mbar, also mb) are units of pressure.
   a. Bar0
   b. Thing
   c. Undefined
   d. Undefined

4. A _____ is a symbolic representation denoting a quantity or expression. It often represents an "unknown" quantity that has the potential to change.
   a. Thing
   b. Variable0
   c. Undefined
   d. Undefined

5. In Euclidean geometry, a _____ is the set of all points in a plane at a fixed distance, called the radius, from a given point, the center.
   a. Thing
   b. Circle0
   c. Undefined
   d. Undefined

6. _____ is a subset of a population.
   a. Sample0
   b. Thing
   c. Undefined
   d. Undefined

7. A bar chart, also known as a _____, is a chart with rectangular bars of lengths usually proportional to the magnitudes or frequencies of what they represent.
   a. Bar graph0
   b. Thing
   c. Undefined
   d. Undefined

8. An _____ is a straight line around which a geometric figure can be rotated.
   a. Thing
   b. Axis0
   c. Undefined
   d. Undefined

9. In astronomy, geography, geometry and related sciences and contexts, a plane is said to be _____ at a given point if it is locally perpendicular to the gradient of the gravity field, i.e., with the direction of the gravitational force at that point.
   a. Thing
   b. Horizontal0
   c. Undefined
   d. Undefined

10. _____ is a kind of property which exists as magnitude or multitude. It is among the basic classes of things along with quality, substance, change, and relation.

Chapter 5. Graphing Linear Equations and Inequalities

a. Thing
b. Amount0
c. Undefined
d. Undefined

11. In Euclidean geometry, a uniform _____ is a linear transformation that enlargers or diminishes objects, and whose _____ factor is the same in all directions. This is also called homothethy.
   a. Scale0
   b. Thing
   c. Undefined
   d. Undefined

12. In sociology and biology a _____ is the collection of people or organisms of a particular species living in a given geographic area or space, usually measured by a census.
   a. Thing
   b. Population0
   c. Undefined
   d. Undefined

13. The word _____ comes from the Latin word linearis, which means created by lines.
   a. Thing
   b. Linear0
   c. Undefined
   d. Undefined

14. A _____ is an equation in which each term is either a constant or the product of a constant times the first power of a variable.
   a. Thing
   b. Linear equation0
   c. Undefined
   d. Undefined

15. In mathematics, an _____ is a statement about the relative size or order of two objects.
   a. Thing
   b. Inequality0
   c. Undefined
   d. Undefined

16. The _____, the average in everyday English, which is also called the arithmetic _____ (and is distinguished from the geometric _____ or harmonic _____). The average is also called the sample _____. The expected value of a random variable, which is also called the population _____.
   a. Thing
   b. Mean0
   c. Undefined
   d. Undefined

17. In business, particularly accounting, a _____ is the time intervals that the accounts, statement, payments, or other calculations cover.
   a. Thing
   b. Period0
   c. Undefined
   d. Undefined

18. In geometry, a line _____ is a part of a line that is bounded by two end points, and contains every point on the line between its end points.
   a. Segment0
   b. Concept
   c. Undefined
   d. Undefined

19. A _____ is the sum of the elements of a sequence.
   a. Thing
   b. Series0
   c. Undefined
   d. Undefined

Chapter 5. Graphing Linear Equations and Inequalities

20. The _____ of measurement are a globally standardized and modernized form of the metric system.
    a. Units0
    b. Thing
    c. Undefined
    d. Undefined

21. A _____ is a set of numbers that designate location in a given reference system, such as x,y in a planar _____ system or an x,y,z in a three-dimensional _____ system.
    a. Coordinate0
    b. Thing
    c. Undefined
    d. Undefined

22. _____ means of or relating to the French philosopher and mathematician René Descartes.
    a. Cartesian0
    b. Thing
    c. Undefined
    d. Undefined

23. A _____ is a part of a line that is bounded by two end points, and contains every point on the line between its end points.
    a. Line segment0
    b. Thing
    c. Undefined
    d. Undefined

24. Acid _____ ratio measures the ability of a company to use its near cash or quick assets to immediately extinguish its current liabilities.
    a. Thing
    b. Test0
    c. Undefined
    d. Undefined

25. In mathematical analysis, _____ are objects which generalize functions and probability distributions.
    a. Thing
    b. Distribution0
    c. Undefined
    d. Undefined

26. In mathematics and the mathematical sciences, a _____ is a fixed, but possibly unspecified, value. This is in contrast to a variable, which is not fixed.
    a. Thing
    b. Constant0
    c. Undefined
    d. Undefined

27. A _____ is a special kind of ratio, indicating a relationship between two measurements with different units, such as miles to gallons or cents to pounds.
    a. Thing
    b. Rate0
    c. Undefined
    d. Undefined

28. In mathematics, _____ expressions is used to reduce the expression into the lowest possible term.
    a. Simplifying0
    b. Thing
    c. Undefined
    d. Undefined

29. An _____ is a collection of two not necessarily distinct objects, one of which is distinguished as the first coordinate and the other as the second coordinate.
    a. Thing
    b. Ordered pair0
    c. Undefined
    d. Undefined

Chapter 5. Graphing Linear Equations and Inequalities

30. _____, either of the curved-bracket punctuation marks that together make a set of _____
    a. Parentheses0
    b. Thing
    c. Undefined
    d. Undefined

31. In mathematics, the conjugate _____ or adjoint matrix of an m-by-n matrix A with complex entries is the n-by-m matrix A* obtained from A by taking the transpose and then taking the complex conjugate of each entry.
    a. Thing
    b. Pairs0
    c. Undefined
    d. Undefined

32. _____ the expected value of a random variable displays the average or central value of the variable. It is a summary value of the distribution of the variable.
    a. Determining0
    b. Thing
    c. Undefined
    d. Undefined

33. A _____ is a one-dimensional picture in which the integers are shown as specially-marked points evenly spaced on a line.
    a. Thing
    b. Number line0
    c. Undefined
    d. Undefined

34. In mathematics and its applications, a _____ is a system for assigning an n-tuple of numbers or scalars to each point in an n-dimensional space.
    a. Coordinate system0
    b. Concept
    c. Undefined
    d. Undefined

35. In mathematics, the _____ of two sets A and B is the set that contains all elements of A that also belong to B (or equivalently, all elements of B that also belong to A), but no other elements.
    a. Thing
    b. Intersection0
    c. Undefined
    d. Undefined

36. An _____ is when two lines intersect somewhere on a plane creating a right angle at intersection
    a. Axes0
    b. Thing
    c. Undefined
    d. Undefined

37. In mathematics, the _____ of a coordinate system is the point where the axes of the system intersect.
    a. Thing
    b. Origin0
    c. Undefined
    d. Undefined

38. A _____ consists of one quarter of the coordinate plane.
    a. Thing
    b. Quadrant0
    c. Undefined
    d. Undefined

39. _____ was a highly influential French philosopher, mathematician, scientist, and writer. Dubbed the "Founder of Modern Philosophy", and the "Father of Modern Mathematics". His theories provided the basis for the calculus of Newton and Leibniz, by applying infinitesimal calculus to the tangent line problem, thus permitting the evolution of that branch of modern mathematics

Chapter 5. Graphing Linear Equations and Inequalities

   a. Person
   c. Undefined
   b. Descartes0
   d. Undefined

40. In geometry, two lines or planes if one falls on the other in such a way as to create congruent adjacent angles. The term may be used as a noun or adjective. Thus, referring to Figure 1, the line AB is the _____ to CD through the point B.
   a. Thing
   c. Undefined
   b. Perpendicular0
   d. Undefined

41. _____ is a synonym for information.
   a. Thing
   c. Undefined
   b. Data0
   d. Undefined

42. A _____ is a simplified and structured visual representation of concepts, ideas, constructions, relations, statistical data, anatomy etc used in all aspects of human activities to visualize and clarify the topic.
   a. Diagram0
   c. Undefined
   b. Thing
   d. Undefined

43. An _____ is an increase, either of some fixed amount, for example added regularly, or of a variable amount.
   a. Increment0
   c. Undefined
   b. Thing
   d. Undefined

44. Transport or _____ is the movement of people and goods from one place to another.
   a. Thing
   c. Undefined
   b. Transportation0
   d. Undefined

45. _____ mathematical functions take numeric arguments and produce numeric results.
   a. Miscellaneous0
   c. Undefined
   b. Thing
   d. Undefined

46. _____ is a way of expressing a number as a fraction of 100 per cent meaning "per hundred".
   a. Thing
   c. Undefined
   b. Percent0
   d. Undefined

47. The population _____ is the total number of human beings alive on the planet Earth at a given time.
   a. Of the world0
   c. Undefined
   b. Thing
   d. Undefined

48. In mathematics, a _____ function in the sense of algebraic geometry is an everywhere-defined, polynomial function on an algebraic variety V with values in the field K over which V is defined.
   a. Regular0
   c. Undefined
   b. Thing
   d. Undefined

49. In mathematics, an _____, mean, or central tendency of a data set refers to a measure of the "middle" or "expected" value of the data set.

a. Average0
b. Concept
c. Undefined
d. Undefined

50. The word _____ is used in a variety of ways in mathematics.
    a. Index0
    b. Thing
    c. Undefined
    d. Undefined

51. _____ is a physical property of a system that underlies the common notions of hot and cold; something that is hotter has the greater _____.
    a. Temperature0
    b. Thing
    c. Undefined
    d. Undefined

52. _____ is the state of being greater than any finite real or natural number, however large.
    a. Thing
    b. Infinite0
    c. Undefined
    d. Undefined

53. A _____ is a set of possible values that a variable can take on in order to satisfy a given set of conditions, which may include equations and inequalities.
    a. Thing
    b. Solution set0
    c. Undefined
    d. Undefined

54. In mathematics, the _____ (or modulus) of a real number is its numerical value without regard to its sign.
    a. Thing
    b. Absolute value0
    c. Undefined
    d. Undefined

55. A _____ of a number is the product of that number with any integer.
    a. Thing
    b. Multiple0
    c. Undefined
    d. Undefined

56. _____ is a notation for writing numbers that is often used by scientists and mathematicians to make it easier to write large and small numbers.
    a. Scientific notation0
    b. Thing
    c. Undefined
    d. Undefined

57. A _____ is the part of a fraction that tells how many equal parts make up a whole, and which is used in the name of the fraction: "halves", "thirds", "fourths" or "quarters", "fifths" and so on.
    a. Denominator0
    b. Concept
    c. Undefined
    d. Undefined

58. In mathematics, a _____ of an integer n, also called a factor of n, is an integer which evenly divides n without leaving a remainder.
    a. Divisor0
    b. Thing
    c. Undefined
    d. Undefined

59. The _____ or kilogramme is the SI base unit of mass. It is defined as being equal to the mass of the international prototype of the _____.

Chapter 5. Graphing Linear Equations and Inequalities

    a. Thing
    c. Undefined
    b. Kilogram0
    d. Undefined

60. In plane geometry, a _____ is a polygon with four equal sides, four right angles, and parallel opposite sides. In algebra, the _____ of a number is that number multiplied by itself.
    a. Square0
    c. Undefined
    b. Thing
    d. Undefined

61. The act of _____ is the calculated approximation of a result which is usable even if input data may be incomplete, uncertain, or noisy.
    a. Thing
    c. Undefined
    b. Estimating0
    d. Undefined

62. In mathematics, a _____ is the result of multiplying, or an expression that identifies factors to be multiplied.
    a. Product0
    c. Undefined
    b. Thing
    d. Undefined

63. In economics _____ means before deductions brutto, e.g. _____ domestic or national product, or _____ profit or income
    a. Thing
    c. Undefined
    b. Gross0
    d. Undefined

64. _____ is the level of functional and/or metabolic efficiency of an organism at both the micro level.
    a. Thing
    c. Undefined
    b. Health0
    d. Undefined

65. A _____ is a unit of length, usually used to measure distance, in a number of different systems, including Imperial units, United States customary units and Norwegian/Swedish mil. Its size can vary from system to system, but in each is between 1 and 10 kilometers. In contemporary English contexts _____ refers to either:
    a. Thing
    c. Undefined
    b. Mile0
    d. Undefined

66. U.S. liquid _____ is legally defined as 231 cubic inches, and is equal to 3.785411784 litres or abotu 0.13368 cubic feet. This is the most common definition of a _____. The U.S. fluid ounce is defined as 1/128 of a U.S. _____.
    a. Thing
    c. Undefined
    b. Gallon0
    d. Undefined

67. The payment of _____ as remuneration for services rendered or products sold is a common way to reward sales people.
    a. Thing
    c. Undefined
    b. Commission0
    d. Undefined

68. _____ of an object is its speed in a particular direction.

a. Thing
b. Velocity0
c. Undefined
d. Undefined

69. Initial objects are also called _____, and terminal objects are also called final.
a. Thing
b. Coterminal0
c. Undefined
d. Undefined

70. A _____ is a negotiable instrument instructing a financial institution to pay a specific amount of a specific currency from a specific demand account held in the maker/depositor's name with that institution. Both the maker and payee may be natural persons or legal entities.
a. Check0
b. Thing
c. Undefined
d. Undefined

71. Any point where a graph makes contact with an coordinate axis is called an _____ of the graph
a. Thing
b. Intercept0
c. Undefined
d. Undefined

72. In combinatorial mathematics, a _____ is an un-ordered collection of unique elements.
a. Combination0
b. Concept
c. Undefined
d. Undefined

73. _____ is a unit of speed, expressing the number of international miles covered per hour.
a. Thing
b. Miles per hour0
c. Undefined
d. Undefined

74. In geometry, a _____ is defined as a quadrilateral where all four of its angles are right angles.
a. Rectangle0
b. Thing
c. Undefined
d. Undefined

75. _____ is the distance around a given two-dimensional object. As a general rule, the _____ of a polygon can always be calculated by adding all the length of the sides together. So, the formula for triangles is P = a + b + c, where a, b and c stand for each side of it. For quadrilaterals the equation is P = a + b + c + d. For equilateral polygons, P = na, where n is the number of sides and a is the side length.
a. Thing
b. Perimeter0
c. Undefined
d. Undefined

76. _____ is the amount of time someone works beyond normal working hours.
a. Compensatory time0
b. Thing
c. Undefined
d. Undefined

77. Mathematical _____ is used to represent ideas.
a. Notation0
b. Thing
c. Undefined
d. Undefined

78. A _____ is a number, figure, or indicator that appears below the normal line of type, typically used in a formula, mathematical expression, or description of a chemical compound.

Chapter 5. Graphing Linear Equations and Inequalities

a. Subscript0
b. Thing
c. Undefined
d. Undefined

79. _____ is often used to describe the measurement of the steepness, incline, gradient, or grade of a straight line. The _____ is defined as the ratio of the "rise" divided by the "run" between two points on a line, or in other words, the ratio of the altitude change to the horizontal distance between any two points on the line.
    a. Thing
    b. Slope0
    c. Undefined
    d. Undefined

80. A _____ is a numeral used to indicate a count. The most common use of the word today is to name the part of a fraction that tells the number or count of equal parts.
    a. Numerator0
    b. Thing
    c. Undefined
    d. Undefined

81. In mathematics, defined and _____ are used to explain whether or not expressions have meaningful, sensible, and unambiguous values.
    a. Undefined0
    b. Thing
    c. Undefined
    d. Undefined

82. A _____ is a landform that extends above the surrounding terrain in a limited area. A _____ is generally steeper than a hill, but there is no universally accepted standard definition for the height of a _____ or a hill although a _____ usually has an identifiable summit.
    a. Thing
    b. Mountain0
    c. Undefined
    d. Undefined

83. In mathematics, a _____ is a constant multiplicative factor of a certain object. The object can be such things as a variable, a vector, a function, etc. For example, the _____ of $9x^2$ is 9.
    a. Thing
    b. Coefficient0
    c. Undefined
    d. Undefined

84. In mathematics, a _____ is a two-dimensional manifold or surface that is perfectly flat.
    a. Thing
    b. Plane0
    c. Undefined
    d. Undefined

85. The existence and properties of _____ are the basis of Euclid's parallel postulate. _____ are two lines on the same plane that do not intersect even assuming that lines extend to infinity in either direction.
    a. Thing
    b. Parallel lines0
    c. Undefined
    d. Undefined

86. In geometry and trigonometry, a _____ is defined as an angle between two straight intersecting lines of ninety degrees, or one-quarter of a circle.
    a. Right angle0
    b. Thing
    c. Undefined
    d. Undefined

87. _____ is a form of periodic payment from an employer to an employee, which is specified in an employment contract.

a. Thing
c. Undefined
b. Gross pay0
d. Undefined

88. A _____ is a form of periodic payment from an employer to an employee, which is specified in an employment contract.
    a. Thing
    b. Salary0
    c. Undefined
    d. Undefined

89. A _____ is a quantity that denotes the proportional amount or magnitude of one quantity relative to another.
    a. Ratio0
    b. Thing
    c. Undefined
    d. Undefined

90. In mathematics, and in particular in abstract algebra, the _____ is a property of binary operations that generalises the distributive law from elementary algebra.
    a. Thing
    b. Distributive property0
    c. Undefined
    d. Undefined

91. In mathematics, the multiplicative inverse of a number x, denoted 1/x or x^{-1}, is the number which, when multiplied by x, yields 1. The multiplicative inverse of x is also called the _____ of x.
    a. Reciprocal0
    b. Thing
    c. Undefined
    d. Undefined

92. In geometry, the _____ of an object is a point in some sense in the middle of the object.
    a. Thing
    b. Center0
    c. Undefined
    d. Undefined

93. In common philosophical language, a proposition or _____, is the content of an assertion, that is, it is true-or-false and defined by the meaning of a particular piece of language.
    a. Statement0
    b. Concept
    c. Undefined
    d. Undefined

94. Two mathematical objects are equal if and only if they are precisely the same in every way. This defines a binary relation, _____, denoted by the sign of _____ "=" in such a way that the statement "x = y" means that x and y are equal.
    a. Equality0
    b. Thing
    c. Undefined
    d. Undefined

95. In mathematics, the additive inverse, or _____ of a number n is the number that, when added to n, yields zero. The additive inverse of n is denoted −n. For example, 7 is −7, because 7 + (−7) = 0, and the additive inverse of −0.3 is 0.3, because −0.3 + 0.3 = 0.
    a. Opposite0
    b. Thing
    c. Undefined
    d. Undefined

96. In mathematics, the _____ of a number n is the number that, when added to n, yields zero. The _____ of n is denoted −n. For example, 7 is −7, because 7 + (−7) = 0, and the _____ of −0.3 is 0.3, because −0.3 + 0.3 = 0.

Chapter 5. Graphing Linear Equations and Inequalities

    a. Thing
    b. Additive inverse0
    c. Undefined
    d. Undefined

97. In mathematics, _____ geometry was the traditional name for the geometry of three-dimensional Euclidean space — for practical purposes the kind of space we live in.
    a. Thing
    b. Solid0
    c. Undefined
    d. Undefined

98. In mathematics, an inequality is a statement about the relative size or order of two objects. For example 14 > 10, or 14 is _____ 10.
    a. Greater than0
    b. Thing
    c. Undefined
    d. Undefined

99. In geometry, _____ lines are two lines that share one or more common points.
    a. Thing
    b. Intersecting0
    c. Undefined
    d. Undefined

100. _____, from Latin meaning "to make progress", is defined in two different ways. Pure economic _____ is the increase in wealth that an investor has from making an investment, taking into consideration all costs associated with that investment including the opportunity cost of capital.
    a. Thing
    b. Profit0
    c. Undefined
    d. Undefined

101. _____ is the application of tools and a processing medium to the transformation of raw materials into finished goods for sale.
    a. Manufacturing0
    b. Thing
    c. Undefined
    d. Undefined

102. The mathematical concept of a _____ expresses the intuitive idea of deterministic dependence between two quantities, one of which is viewed as primary and the other as secondary. A _____ then is a way to associate a unique output for each input of a specified type, for example, a real number or an element of a given set.
    a. Thing
    b. Function0
    c. Undefined
    d. Undefined

103. An _____ or member of a set is an object that when collected together make up the set.
    a. Element0
    b. Thing
    c. Undefined
    d. Undefined

104. In mathematics, the _____ , or members of a set or more generally a class are all those objects which when collected together make up the set or class.
    a. Elements0
    b. Thing
    c. Undefined
    d. Undefined

105. In mathematics, in the field of group theory, a _____ of a group is a quasisimple subnormal subgroup.

a. Concept
b. Component0
c. Undefined
d. Undefined

106. In mathematics, the _____ of a function is the set of all "output" values produced by that function. Given a function $f : A \to B$, the _____ of f, is defined to be the set $\{x \in B : x = f(a) \text{ for some } a \in A\}$.
   a. Range0
   b. Thing
   c. Undefined
   d. Undefined

107. In mathematics, a _____ of a k-place relation $L \subseteq X_1 \times \ldots \times X_k$ is one of the sets X_j, $1 \leq j \leq k$. In the special case where k = 2 and $L \subseteq X_1 \times X_2$ is a function $L : X_1 \to X_2$, it is conventional to refer to X_1 as the _____ of the function and to refer to X_2 as the codomain of the function.
   a. Domain0
   b. Thing
   c. Undefined
   d. Undefined

108. In mathematics, an _____ is any of the arguments, i.e. "inputs", to a function. Thus if we have a function f(x), then x is a _____.
   a. Thing
   b. Independent variable0
   c. Undefined
   d. Undefined

109. In a function the _____, is the variable which is the value, i.e. the "output", of the function.
   a. Thing
   b. Dependent variable0
   c. Undefined
   d. Undefined

110. In mathematics, the _____ f is the collection of all ordered pairs . In particular, graph means the graphical representation of this collection, in the form of a curve or surface, together with axes, etc. Graphing on a Cartesian plane is sometimes referred to as curve sketching.
   a. Graph of a function0
   b. Thing
   c. Undefined
   d. Undefined

111. Equivalence is the condition of being _____ or essentially equal.
   a. Equivalent0
   b. Thing
   c. Undefined
   d. Undefined

112. _____ are objects, characters, or other concrete representations of ideas, concepts, or other abstractions.
   a. Symbols0
   b. Thing
   c. Undefined
   d. Undefined

113. _____ is a branch of mathematics concerning the study of structure, relation and quantity.
   a. Concept
   b. Algebra0
   c. Undefined
   d. Undefined

114. _____ is a test to determine if a relation or its graph is a function or not
   a. Thing
   b. Vertical line test0
   c. Undefined
   d. Undefined

115. A _____ is a compensation which workers receive in exchange for their labor.

Chapter 5. Graphing Linear Equations and Inequalities

a. Wage0
b. Thing
c. Undefined
d. Undefined

116. _____ is change in population over time, and can be quantified as the change in the number of individuals in a population per unit time.
   a. Thing
   b. Population growth0
   c. Undefined
   d. Undefined

117. Fixed costs are expenses whose total does not change in proportion to the activity of a business.Unit fixed costs decline with volume following a retangular hyperbola as the volume of production.Variable costs by contrast change in relation to the activity of a business such as sales or production volume.Along with variable costs,fixed costs make up one of the two components of total cost. In the most simple production function total cost is equal to fixed costs plus variable costs.In accounting terminology, fixed costs will broadly include all costs which are not included in cost of goods sold, and variable costs are those captured in costs of goods sold. The implicit assumption required to make the equivalence between the accounting and economics terminology is that the accounting period is equal to the period in which fixed costs do not vary in relation to production. In practice, this equivalence does not always hold and depending on the period under consideration by management, some overhead expenses can be adjusted by management, and the specific allocation of each expense to each category will be decided under cost accounting.In business planning and management accounting, usage of the terms fixed costs, variable costs and others will often differ from usage in economics, and may depend on the intended use. For example, costs may be segregated into per unit costs fixed costs per period, and variable costs as a proportion of revenue. Capital expenditures will usually be allocated separately, and depending on the purpose, a portion may be regularly allocated to expenses as depreciation and amortization and seen as a _____ per period, or the entire amount may be considered upfront fixed costs.
   a. Fixed cost0
   b. Thing
   c. Undefined
   d. Undefined

118. _____ is the general term that is used to describe physical artifacts of a technology.
   a. Thing
   b. Hardware0
   c. Undefined
   d. Undefined

Chapter 6. Systems of Linear Equations

1. An _____ is a collection of two not necessarily distinct objects, one of which is distinguished as the first coordinate and the other as the second coordinate.
   a. Ordered pair0
   b. Thing
   c. Undefined
   d. Undefined

2. A _____ is a set of numbers that designate location in a given reference system, such as x,y in a planar _____ system or an x,y,z in a three-dimensional _____ system.
   a. Thing
   b. Coordinate0
   c. Undefined
   d. Undefined

3. A _____ is a symbolic representation denoting a quantity or expression. It often represents an "unknown" quantity that has the potential to change.
   a. Variable0
   b. Thing
   c. Undefined
   d. Undefined

4. The word _____ comes from the Latin word linearis, which means created by lines.
   a. Thing
   b. Linear0
   c. Undefined
   d. Undefined

5. A _____ is an equation in which each term is either a constant or the product of a constant times the first power of a variable.
   a. Linear equation0
   b. Thing
   c. Undefined
   d. Undefined

6. _____ is the state of being greater than any finite real or natural number, however large.
   a. Thing
   b. Infinite0
   c. Undefined
   d. Undefined

7. In mathematics, the conjugate _____ or adjoint matrix of an m-by-n matrix A with complex entries is the n-by-m matrix A* obtained from A by taking the transpose and then taking the complex conjugate of each entry.
   a. Pairs0
   b. Thing
   c. Undefined
   d. Undefined

8. _____ the expected value of a random variable displays the average or central value of the variable. It is a summary value of the distribution of the variable.
   a. Thing
   b. Determining0
   c. Undefined
   d. Undefined

9. _____ are the basic objects of study in graph theory. Informally speaking, a graph is a set of objects called points, nodes, or vertices connected by links called lines or edges.
   a. Thing
   b. Graphs0
   c. Undefined
   d. Undefined

10. In mathematics, the _____ of two sets A and B is the set that contains all elements of A that also belong to B (or equivalently, all elements of B that also belong to A), but no other elements.

Chapter 6. Systems of Linear Equations

a. Thing
c. Undefined
b. Intersection0
d. Undefined

11. In mathematics and its applications, a _____ is a system for assigning an n-tuple of numbers or scalars to each point in an n-dimensional space.
a. Concept
c. Undefined
b. Coordinate system0
d. Undefined

12. A _____ is a negotiable instrument instructing a financial institution to pay a specific amount of a specific currency from a specific demand account held in the maker/depositor's name with that institution. Both the maker and payee may be natural persons or legal entities.
a. Check0
c. Undefined
b. Thing
d. Undefined

13. _____ are a set of equations containing multiple variables.
a. Thing
c. Undefined
b. Systems of equations0
d. Undefined

14. The _____ are the only integral domain whose positive elements are well-ordered, and in which order is preserved by addition. Like the natural numbers, the _____ form a countably infinite set. The set of all _____ is usually denoted in mathematics by a boldface Z .
a. Thing
c. Undefined
b. Integers0
d. Undefined

15. The existence and properties of _____ are the basis of Euclid's parallel postulate. _____ are two lines on the same plane that do not intersect even assuming that lines extend to infinity in either direction.
a. Thing
c. Undefined
b. Parallel lines0
d. Undefined

16. A _____ of a number is the product of that number with any integer.
a. Thing
c. Undefined
b. Multiple0
d. Undefined

17. In mathematics and the mathematical sciences, a _____ is a fixed, but possibly unspecified, value. This is in contrast to a variable, which is not fixed.
a. Thing
c. Undefined
b. Constant0
d. Undefined

18. _____ is often used to describe the measurement of the steepness, incline, gradient, or grade of a straight line. The _____ is defined as the ratio of the "rise" divided by the "run" between two points on a line, or in other words, the ratio of the altitude change to the horizontal distance between any two points on the line.
a. Slope0
c. Undefined
b. Thing
d. Undefined

19. In mathematics, a _____ is a two-dimensional manifold or surface that is perfectly flat.

63

Chapter 6. Systems of Linear Equations

a. Plane0
b. Thing
c. Undefined
d. Undefined

20. In mathematics, and in particular in abstract algebra, the _____ is a property of binary operations that generalises the distributive law from elementary algebra.
    a. Distributive property0
    b. Thing
    c. Undefined
    d. Undefined

21. Two mathematical objects are equal if and only if they are precisely the same in every way. This defines a binary relation, _____, denoted by the sign of _____ "=" in such a way that the statement "x = y" means that x and y are equal.
    a. Thing
    b. Equality0
    c. Undefined
    d. Undefined

22. Equivalence is the condition of being _____ or essentially equal.
    a. Thing
    b. Equivalent0
    c. Undefined
    d. Undefined

23. A _____ is the result of the addition of a set of numbers. The numbers may be natural numbers, complex numbers, matrices, or still more complicated objects. An infinite _____ is a subtle procedure known as a series.
    a. Thing
    b. Sum0
    c. Undefined
    d. Undefined

24. In mathematics, a _____ is a constant multiplicative factor of a certain object. The object can be such things as a variable, a vector, a function, etc. For example, the _____ of $9x^2$ is 9.
    a. Thing
    b. Coefficient0
    c. Undefined
    d. Undefined

25. In mathematics, the additive inverse, or _____ of a number n is the number that, when added to n, yields zero. The additive inverse of n is denoted −n. For example, 7 is −7, because 7 + (−7) = 0, and the additive inverse of −0.3 is 0.3, because −0.3 + 0.3 = 0.
    a. Thing
    b. Opposite0
    c. Undefined
    d. Undefined

26. _____ element of an element x with respect to a binary operation * with identity element e is an element y such that x * y = y * x = e. In particular,
    a. Inverse0
    b. Thing
    c. Undefined
    d. Undefined

27. In mathematics, the _____ inverse, or opposite, of a number n is the number that, when added to n, yields zero. The _____ inverse of n is denoted −n.
    a. Additive0
    b. Thing
    c. Undefined
    d. Undefined

28. In mathematics, the _____ of a number n is the number that, when added to n, yields zero. The _____ of n is denoted −n. For example, 7 is −7, because 7 + (−7) = 0, and the _____ of −0.3 is 0.3, because −0.3 + 0.3 = 0.

Chapter 6. Systems of Linear Equations

    a. Additive inverse0
    b. Thing
    c. Undefined
    d. Undefined

29. In common philosophical language, a proposition or _____, is the content of an assertion, that is, it is true-or-false and defined by the meaning of a particular piece of language.
    a. Statement0
    b. Concept
    c. Undefined
    d. Undefined

30. The _____, the average in everyday English, which is also called the arithmetic _____ (and is distinguished from the geometric _____ or harmonic _____). The average is also called the sample _____. The expected value of a random variable, which is also called the population _____.
    a. Thing
    b. Mean0
    c. Undefined
    d. Undefined

31. An _____ is a combination of numbers, operators, grouping symbols and/or free variables and bound variables arranged in a meaningful way which can be evaluated..
    a. Thing
    b. Expression0
    c. Undefined
    d. Undefined

32. In mathematics, _____ is an elementary arithmetic operation. When one of the numbers is a whole number, _____ is the repeated sum of the other number.
    a. Multiplication0
    b. Thing
    c. Undefined
    d. Undefined

33. The _____ is used to discard one of the variables in an equation, only to replace it with the actual value when solving multiple equations.
    a. Substitution method0
    b. Thing
    c. Undefined
    d. Undefined

34. In mathematics, _____ are essentially word problems that are designed to use mathematical critical thinking in everyday situations.
    a. Application problems0
    b. Thing
    c. Undefined
    d. Undefined

35. _____ is a kind of property which exists as magnitude or multitude. It is among the basic classes of things along with quality, substance, change, and relation.
    a. Amount0
    b. Thing
    c. Undefined
    d. Undefined

36. U.S. liquid _____ is legally defined as 231 cubic inches, and is equal to 3.785411784 litres or abotu 0.13368 cubic feet. This is the most common definition of a _____. The U.S. fluid ounce is defined as 1/128 of a U.S. _____.
    a. Gallon0
    b. Thing
    c. Undefined
    d. Undefined

37. In mathematics, a _____ or rhodonea curve is a sinusoid plotted in polar coordinates.

Chapter 6. Systems of Linear Equations

a. Rose0
b. Thing
c. Undefined
d. Undefined

38. _____ usually refers to money in the form of liquid currency, such as banknotes or coins.
    a. Thing
    b. Cash0
    c. Undefined
    d. Undefined

39. A _____ is a special kind of ratio, indicating a relationship between two measurements with different units, such as miles to gallons or cents to pounds.
    a. Rate0
    b. Thing
    c. Undefined
    d. Undefined

40. A _____ is a unit of length in the metric system, equal to one thousand metres, the current SI base unit of length
    a. Kilometer0
    b. Thing
    c. Undefined
    d. Undefined

41. The plus and _____ signs are mathematical symbols used to represent the notions of positive and negative as well as the operations of addition and subtraction.
    a. Thing
    b. Minus0
    c. Undefined
    d. Undefined

42. In mathematics, an _____, mean, or central tendency of a data set refers to a measure of the "middle" or "expected" value of the data set.
    a. Concept
    b. Average0
    c. Undefined
    d. Undefined

43. A _____ is a unit of length, usually used to measure distance, in a number of different systems, including Imperial units, United States customary units and Norwegian/Swedish mil. Its size can vary from system to system, but in each is between 1 and 10 kilometers. In contemporary English contexts _____ refers to either:
    a. Thing
    b. Mile0
    c. Undefined
    d. Undefined

44. _____ is a unit of speed, expressing the number of international miles covered per hour.
    a. Miles per hour0
    b. Thing
    c. Undefined
    d. Undefined

45. _____ is the transport of people on a trip/journey or the process or time involved in a person or object moving from one location to another.
    a. Travel0
    b. Thing
    c. Undefined
    d. Undefined

46. _____ is the fee paid on borrowed money.
    a. Thing
    b. Interest0
    c. Undefined
    d. Undefined

Chapter 6. Systems of Linear Equations

47. In chemistry, a _____ is substance made by combining two or more different materials in such a way that no chemical reaction occurs.
    a. Thing
    b. Mixture0
    c. Undefined
    d. Undefined

48. Regrouping is the act of putting ones into groups of 10. For example, the 1 on the far right of 131 would be denoted _____ if the digit of the number being subtracted is larger than 1, such as 131-99.
    a. By 100
    b. Thing
    c. Undefined
    d. Undefined

49. The population _____ is the total number of human beings alive on the planet Earth at a given time.
    a. Thing
    b. Of the world0
    c. Undefined
    d. Undefined

50. The metre (or _____, see spelling differences) is a measure of length. It is the basic unit of length in the metric system and in the International System of Units (SI), used around the world for general and scientific purposes.
    a. Concept
    b. Meter0
    c. Undefined
    d. Undefined

51. An _____, also called a minor planet or planetoid, comes from a class of atsronomical objects.
    a. Thing
    b. Asteroid0
    c. Undefined
    d. Undefined

52. In geometry, a _____ (Greek words diairo = divide and metro = measure) of a circle is any straight line segment that passes through the centre and whose endpoints are on the circular boundary, or, in more modern usage, the length of such a line segment. When using the word in the more modern sense, one speaks of the _____ rather than a _____, because all diameters of a circle have the same length. This length is twice the radius. The _____ of a circle is also the longest chord that the circle has.
    a. Thing
    b. Diameter0
    c. Undefined
    d. Undefined

53. _____ is electromagnetic radiation with a wavelength that is visible to the eye (visible _____) or, in a technical or scientific context, electromagnetic radiation of any wavelength.
    a. Light0
    b. Thing
    c. Undefined
    d. Undefined

54. In business, _____, _____ cost or _____ expense refers to an ongoing expense of operating a business.
    a. Thing
    b. Overhead0
    c. Undefined
    d. Undefined

55. _____ or life assurance is a contract between the policy owner and the insurer, where the insurer agrees to pay a sum of money upon the occurrence of the policy owner's death.
    a. Life insurance0
    b. Thing
    c. Undefined
    d. Undefined

Chapter 6. Systems of Linear Equations

56. _____, in law and economics, is a form of risk management primarily used to hedge against the risk of a contingent loss.
   a. Thing
   b. Insurance0
   c. Undefined
   d. Undefined

57. A _____ is a method of using property as security for the payment of a debt.
   a. Thing
   b. Mortgage0
   c. Undefined
   d. Undefined

58. _____, also referred to as common or ordinary shares, are, as the name implies, the most usual and commonly held form of stock in a corporation
   a. Thing
   b. Common stock0
   c. Undefined
   d. Undefined

59. A _____ is a numerical performance objective.
   a. Quota0
   b. Thing
   c. Undefined
   d. Undefined

60. _____ is the distance around a given two-dimensional object. As a general rule, the _____ of a polygon can always be calculated by adding all the length of the sides together. So, the formula for triangles is P = a + b + c, where a, b and c stand for each side of it. For quadrilaterals the equation is P = a + b + c + d. For equilateral polygons, P = na, where n is the number of sides and a is the side length.
   a. Thing
   b. Perimeter0
   c. Undefined
   d. Undefined

61. A _____ is a quadrilateral, which is defined as a shape with four sides, which has a pair of parallel sides.
   a. Trapezoid0
   b. Thing
   c. Undefined
   d. Undefined

62. A pair of angles is _____ if their respective measures sum to 180 degrees.
   a. Concept
   b. Supplementary0
   c. Undefined
   d. Undefined

63. A _____ is a function that assigns a number to subsets of a given set.
   a. Measure0
   b. Thing
   c. Undefined
   d. Undefined

64. A pair of angles are _____ if the sum of their angles is 90°.
   a. Complementary0
   b. Concept
   c. Undefined
   d. Undefined

65. In mathematics, an _____ is a statement about the relative size or order of two objects.
   a. Inequality0
   b. Thing
   c. Undefined
   d. Undefined

Chapter 6. Systems of Linear Equations

66. In mathematics, _____ geometry was the traditional name for the geometry of three-dimensional Euclidean space — for practical purposes the kind of space we live in.
    a. Thing
    b. Solid0
    c. Undefined
    d. Undefined

67. Acid _____ ratio measures the ability of a company to use its near cash or quick assets to immediately extinguish its current liabilities.
    a. Thing
    b. Test0
    c. Undefined
    d. Undefined

68. In mathematics, the _____ of a coordinate system is the point where the axes of the system intersect.
    a. Origin0
    b. Thing
    c. Undefined
    d. Undefined

69. An _____ is when two lines intersect somewhere on a plane creating a right angle at intersection
    a. Thing
    b. Axes0
    c. Undefined
    d. Undefined

70. A _____ is a form of collective investment that pools money from many investors and invests their money in stocks, bonds, short-term money market instruments, and/or other securities.
    a. Thing
    b. Mutual fund0
    c. Undefined
    d. Undefined

71. _____ finance, in finance, a debt security, issued by Issuer
    a. Thing
    b. Bond0
    c. Undefined
    d. Undefined

72. _____ or arithmetics is the oldest and most elementary branch of mathematics, used by almost everyone, for tasks ranging from simple daily counting to advanced science and business calculations.
    a. Arithmetic0
    b. Thing
    c. Undefined
    d. Undefined

73. In mathematics, factorization (British English: factorisation) or factoring is the decomposition of an object (for example, a number, a polynomial, or a matrix) into a product of other objects, or _____, which when multiplied together give the original.
    a. Factors0
    b. Thing
    c. Undefined
    d. Undefined

74. In mathematics, a _____ number (or a _____) is a natural number that has exactly two (distinct) natural number divisors, which are 1 and the _____ number itself.
    a. Prime0
    b. Thing
    c. Undefined
    d. Undefined

75. The _____ of a positive integer are the prime numbers that divide into that integer exactly, without leaving a remainder. The process of finding these numbers is called integer factorization, or prime factorization.

a. Prime factor0 b. Thing
c. Undefined d. Undefined

76. _____ is a branch of mathematics concerning the study of structure, relation and quantity.
a. Concept b. Algebra0
c. Undefined d. Undefined

77. In mathematics, a _____ is an expression that is constructed from one or more variables and constants, using only the operations of addition, subtraction, multiplication, and constant positive whole number exponents. is a _____. Note in particular that division by an expression containing a variable is not in general allowed in polynomials. [1]
a. Thing b. Polynomial0
c. Undefined d. Undefined

78. In mathematics, a _____ is the result of multiplying, or an expression that identifies factors to be multiplied.
a. Product0 b. Thing
c. Undefined d. Undefined

79. In mathematics, _____ is the decomposition of an object into a product of other objects, or factors, which when multiplied together give the original.
a. Factoring0 b. Thing
c. Undefined d. Undefined

80. In mathematics, a _____ is the end result of a division problem. It can also be expressed as the number of times the divisor divides into the dividend.
a. Thing b. Quotient0
c. Undefined d. Undefined

81. In mathematics, a _____ number is a number which can be expressed as a ratio of two integers. Non-integer _____ numbers (commonly called fractions) are usually written as the vulgar fraction a / b, where b is not zero.
a. Thing b. Rational0
c. Undefined d. Undefined

Chapter 7. Factors, Divisors, and Factoring

1. In mathematics, a _____ of an integer n, also called a factor of n, is an integer which evenly divides n without leaving a remainder.
   a. Thing
   b. Divisor0
   c. Undefined
   d. Undefined

2. In mathematics, _____ is the decomposition of an object into a product of other objects, or factors, which when multiplied together give the original.
   a. Thing
   b. Factoring0
   c. Undefined
   d. Undefined

3. In mathematics, factorization (British English: factorisation) or factoring is the decomposition of an object (for example, a number, a polynomial, or a matrix) into a product of other objects, or _____, which when multiplied together give the original.
   a. Factors0
   b. Thing
   c. Undefined
   d. Undefined

4. In mathematics, a _____ number (or a _____) is a natural number that has exactly two (distinct) natural number divisors, which are 1 and the _____ number itself.
   a. Prime0
   b. Thing
   c. Undefined
   d. Undefined

5. A _____ number is a positive integer which has a positive divisor other than one or itself.
   a. Composite0
   b. Thing
   c. Undefined
   d. Undefined

6. _____ is a positive integer which has a positive divisor other than one or itself.
   a. Thing
   b. Composite numbers0
   c. Undefined
   d. Undefined

7. In mathematics, a _____ can mean either an element of the set {1, 2, 3, ...} (i.e the positive integers or the counting numbers) or an element of the set {0, 1, 2, 3, ...} (i.e. the non-negative integers).
   a. Natural number0
   b. Thing
   c. Undefined
   d. Undefined

8. A _____ is the part of the dividend that is left over when the dividend is not evenly divisible by the divisor.
   a. Remainder0
   b. Thing
   c. Undefined
   d. Undefined

9. A _____ is the result of the addition of a set of numbers. The numbers may be natural numbers, complex numbers, matrices, or still more complicated objects. An infinite _____ is a subtle procedure known as a series.
   a. Thing
   b. Sum0
   c. Undefined
   d. Undefined

10. _____, in number theory is the process of breaking down a composite number into smaller non-trivial divisors, which when multiplied together equal the original integer.

Chapter 7. Factors, Divisors, and Factoring

a. Integer factorization0
b. Thing
c. Undefined
d. Undefined

11. _____ is a natural number that has exactly two distinct natural number divisors, which are 1 and the _____ itself.
a. Prime number0
b. Thing
c. Undefined
d. Undefined

12. In mathematics, a _____ is the end result of a division problem. It can also be expressed as the number of times the divisor divides into the dividend.
a. Quotient0
b. Thing
c. Undefined
d. Undefined

13. In mathematics, a _____ is the result of multiplying, or an expression that identifies factors to be multiplied.
a. Product0
b. Thing
c. Undefined
d. Undefined

14. In mathematics, an inequality is a statement about the relative size or order of two objects. For example 14 > 10, or 14 is _____ 10.
a. Greater than0
b. Thing
c. Undefined
d. Undefined

15. In plane geometry, a _____ is a polygon with four equal sides, four right angles, and parallel opposite sides. In algebra, the _____ of a number is that number multiplied by itself.
a. Square0
b. Thing
c. Undefined
d. Undefined

16. The _____ of a positive integer are the prime numbers that divide into that integer exactly, without leaving a remainder. The process of finding these numbers is called integer factorization, or prime factorization.
a. Prime factor0
b. Thing
c. Undefined
d. Undefined

17. In mathematics, the _____ divisor of two non-zero integers, is the largest positive integer that divides both numbers without remainder.
a. Greatest common0
b. Thing
c. Undefined
d. Undefined

18. In Math the greates common divisor sometimes known as the _____ of two non- zero integers.
a. Greatest common factor0
b. Thing
c. Undefined
d. Undefined

19. _____ is the largest positive integer that divides both numbers without remainder.
a. Thing
b. Common Factor0
c. Undefined
d. Undefined

Chapter 7. Factors, Divisors, and Factoring

20. An _____ is a combination of numbers, operators, grouping symbols and/or free variables and bound variables arranged in a meaningful way which can be evaluated..
    a. Expression0
    b. Thing
    c. Undefined
    d. Undefined

21. _____ has many meanings, most of which simply .
    a. Power0
    b. Thing
    c. Undefined
    d. Undefined

22. _____ is a mathematical operation, written a^n, involving two numbers, the base a and the exponent n.
    a. Thing
    b. Exponentiating0
    c. Undefined
    d. Undefined

23. _____ is a mathematical operation, written a^n, involving two numbers, the base a and the exponent n.
    a. Thing
    b. Exponentiation0
    c. Undefined
    d. Undefined

24. The _____, the average in everyday English, which is also called the arithmetic _____ (and is distinguished from the geometric _____ or harmonic _____). The average is also called the sample _____. The expected value of a random variable, which is also called the population _____.
    a. Mean0
    b. Thing
    c. Undefined
    d. Undefined

25. In mathematics, a _____ is a particular kind of polynomial, having just one term.
    a. Thing
    b. Monomial0
    c. Undefined
    d. Undefined

26. A _____ is a symbolic representation denoting a quantity or expression. It often represents an "unknown" quantity that has the potential to change.
    a. Thing
    b. Variable0
    c. Undefined
    d. Undefined

27. In mathematics, there are several meanings of _____ depending on the subject.
    a. Degree0
    b. Thing
    c. Undefined
    d. Undefined

28. In mathematics, a _____ is an expression that is constructed from one or more variables and constants, using only the operations of addition, subtraction, multiplication, and constant positive whole number exponents. is a _____. Note in particular that division by an expression containing a variable is not in general allowed in polynomials. [1]
    a. Polynomial0
    b. Thing
    c. Undefined
    d. Undefined

29. In elementary algebra, a _____ is a polynomial with two terms: the sum of two monomials. It is the simplest kind of polynomial except for a monomial.

Chapter 7. Factors, Divisors, and Factoring

a. Thing
b. Binomial0
c. Undefined
d. Undefined

30. _____, either of the curved-bracket punctuation marks that together make a set of _____
    a. Thing
    b. Parentheses0
    c. Undefined
    d. Undefined

31. In mathematics, a _____ is a constant multiplicative factor of a certain object. The object can be such things as a variable, a vector, a function, etc. For example, the _____ of $9x^2$ is 9.
    a. Thing
    b. Coefficient0
    c. Undefined
    d. Undefined

32. A _____ is a negotiable instrument instructing a financial institution to pay a specific amount of a specific currency from a specific demand account held in the maker/depositor's name with that institution. Both the maker and payee may be natural persons or legal entities.
    a. Thing
    b. Check0
    c. Undefined
    d. Undefined

33. In mathematics, and in particular in abstract algebra, the _____ is a property of binary operations that generalises the distributive law from elementary algebra.
    a. Thing
    b. Distributive property0
    c. Undefined
    d. Undefined

34. A _____ is a polynomial consisting of three terms; in other words, it is the sum of three monomials.
    a. Thing
    b. Trinomial0
    c. Undefined
    d. Undefined

35. In mathematics, _____ is an elementary arithmetic operation. When one of the numbers is a whole number, _____ is the repeated sum of the other number.
    a. Multiplication0
    b. Thing
    c. Undefined
    d. Undefined

36. In mathematics, the additive inverse, or _____ of a number n is the number that, when added to n, yields zero. The additive inverse of n is denoted −n. For example, 7 is −7, because 7 + (−7) = 0, and the additive inverse of −0.3 is 0.3, because −0.3 + 0.3 = 0.
    a. Thing
    b. Opposite0
    c. Undefined
    d. Undefined

37. In mathematics, the _____ of a number n is the number that, when added to n, yields zero. The _____ of n is denoted −n. For example, 7 is −7, because 7 + (−7) = 0, and the _____ of −0.3 is 0.3, because −0.3 + 0.3 = 0.
    a. Additive inverse0
    b. Thing
    c. Undefined
    d. Undefined

38. In mathematics, the _____ (or modulus) of a real number is its numerical value without regard to its sign.

Chapter 7. Factors, Divisors, and Factoring

    a. Thing   b. Absolute value0
    c. Undefined   d. Undefined

39. In combinatorial mathematics, a _____ is an un-ordered collection of unique elements.
    a. Combination0   b. Concept
    c. Undefined   d. Undefined

40. In mathematics and the mathematical sciences, a _____ is a fixed, but possibly unspecified, value. This is in contrast to a variable, which is not fixed.
    a. Thing   b. Constant0
    c. Undefined   d. Undefined

41. _____ is a fixed, but possibly unspecified, value. This is in contrast to a variable, which is not fixed.
    a. Constant term0   b. Thing
    c. Undefined   d. Undefined

42. In abstract algebra, _____ consists of sets with binary operations that satisfy certain axioms.
    a. Grouping0   b. Thing
    c. Undefined   d. Undefined

43. In mathematics the _____ refers to the identity: $a^2 - b^2 = (a+b)(a-b)$
    a. Difference of two squares0   b. Thing
    c. Undefined   d. Undefined

44. In mathematics, the conjugate _____ or adjoint matrix of an m-by-n matrix A with complex entries is the n-by-m matrix A* obtained from A by taking the transpose and then taking the complex conjugate of each entry.
    a. Pairs0   b. Thing
    c. Undefined   d. Undefined

45. In algebra, a _____ is a binomial formed by taking the opposite of the second term of a binomial.
    a. Conjugate0   b. Thing
    c. Undefined   d. Undefined

46. In mathematics, a matrix can be thought of as each row or _____ being a vector. Hence, a space formed by row vectors or _____ vectors are said to be a row space or a _____ space.
    a. Concept   b. Column0
    c. Undefined   d. Undefined

47. _____ is a concept that permeates much of inferential statistics and descriptive statistics. More properly, it is "the sum of the squared deviations".
    a. Sum of squares0   b. Thing
    c. Undefined   d. Undefined

48. A _____ is a three-dimensional solid object bounded by six square faces, facets, or sides, with three meeting at each vertex.

a. Cube0
b. Thing
c. Undefined
d. Undefined

49. _____ are of a number n in its third power-the result of multiplying it by itself three times.
   a. Cubes0
   b. Thing
   c. Undefined
   d. Undefined

50. The _____ are the only integral domain whose positive elements are well-ordered, and in which order is preserved by addition. Like the natural numbers, the _____ form a countably infinite set. The set of all _____ is usually denoted in mathematics by a boldface Z .
   a. Thing
   b. Integers0
   c. Undefined
   d. Undefined

51. The term _____ can refer to an integer which is the square of some other integer, or an algebraic expression that can be factored as the square of some other expression.
   a. Perfect square0
   b. Thing
   c. Undefined
   d. Undefined

52. _____ is a branch of mathematics concerning the study of structure, relation and quantity.
   a. Concept
   b. Algebra0
   c. Undefined
   d. Undefined

53. The word _____ comes from the Latin word linearis, which means created by lines.
   a. Thing
   b. Linear0
   c. Undefined
   d. Undefined

54. A _____ is an equation in which each term is either a constant or the product of a constant times the first power of a variable.
   a. Thing
   b. Linear equation0
   c. Undefined
   d. Undefined

55. A _____ is one of the basic shapes of geometry: a polygon with three vertices and three sides which are straight line segments.
   a. Thing
   b. Triangle0
   c. Undefined
   d. Undefined

56. In geometry, a _____ is defined as a quadrilateral where all four of its angles are right angles.
   a. Rectangle0
   b. Thing
   c. Undefined
   d. Undefined

57. _____ means in succession or back-to-back
   a. Thing
   b. Consecutive0
   c. Undefined
   d. Undefined

58. In arithmetic and algebra, when a number or expression is both preceded and followed by a binary operation, an _____ is required for which operation should be applied first.

a. Order of operations0
b. Thing
c. Undefined
d. Undefined

59. Two mathematical objects are equal if and only if they are precisely the same in every way. This defines a binary relation, _____, denoted by the sign of _____ "=" in such a way that the statement "x = y" means that x and y are equal.
   a. Thing
   b. Equality0
   c. Undefined
   d. Undefined

60. In mathematics, a _____ is a polynomial equation of the second degree. The general form is $ax^2 + bx + c = 0$.
   a. Thing
   b. Quadratic equation0
   c. Undefined
   d. Undefined

61. _____ also known as the zero-product rule, is an abstract and explicit statement of the familiar property from elementary mathematics that if the product of two real numbers is zero, then at least one of the numbers in the product factors must be zero.
   a. Thing
   b. Zero product property0
   c. Undefined
   d. Undefined

62. _____ are the basic objects of study in graph theory. Informally speaking, a graph is a set of objects called points, nodes, or vertices connected by links called lines or edges.
   a. Thing
   b. Graphs0
   c. Undefined
   d. Undefined

63. In mathematics, the _____ is a conic section generated by the intersection of a right circular conical surface and a plane parallel to a generating straight line of that surface. It can also be defined as locus of points in a plane which are equidistant from a given point.
   a. Parabola0
   b. Thing
   c. Undefined
   d. Undefined

64. _____ of an object is its speed in a particular direction.
   a. Velocity0
   b. Thing
   c. Undefined
   d. Undefined

65. Initial objects are also called _____, and terminal objects are also called final.
   a. Coterminal0
   b. Thing
   c. Undefined
   d. Undefined

66. _____, in economics and political economy, are the distributions or payments awarded to the various suppliers of the factors of production.
   a. Thing
   b. Returns0
   c. Undefined
   d. Undefined

67. A _____ can refer to a line joining two nonadjacent vertices of a polygon or polyhedron, or in some contexts any upward or downward sloping line. .

Chapter 7. Factors, Divisors, and Factoring

a. Thing
b. Diagonal0
c. Undefined
d. Undefined

68. A _____ is a number that is less than zero.
a. Negative number0
b. Thing
c. Undefined
d. Undefined

69. In geometry, a _____ is a special kind of point, usually a corner of a polygon, polyhedron, or higher dimensional polytope. In the geometry of curves a _____ is a point of where the first derivative of curvature is zero. In graph theory, a _____ is the fundamental unit out of which graphs are formed
a. Vertex0
b. Thing
c. Undefined
d. Undefined

70. In geometry a _____ is a plane figure that is bounded by a closed path or circuit, composed of a finite number of sequential line segments.
a. Thing
b. Polygon0
c. Undefined
d. Undefined

71. A _____ is a polynomial function of the form $f(x) = ax^2 + bx + c$, where a, b, c are real numbers and a , 0.
a. Event
b. Quadratic function0
c. Undefined
d. Undefined

72. The mathematical concept of a _____ expresses the intuitive idea of deterministic dependence between two quantities, one of which is viewed as primary and the other as secondary. A _____ then is a way to associate a unique output for each input of a specified type, for example, a real number or an element of a given set.
a. Thing
b. Function0
c. Undefined
d. Undefined

73. In mathematical analysis and related areas of mathematics, a set is called _____, if it is, in a certain sense, of finite size.
a. Bounded0
b. Thing
c. Undefined
d. Undefined

74. A _____ is a unit of length, usually used to measure distance, in a number of different systems, including Imperial units, United States customary units and Norwegian/Swedish mil. Its size can vary from system to system, but in each is between 1 and 10 kilometers. In contemporary English contexts _____ refers to either:
a. Mile0
b. Thing
c. Undefined
d. Undefined

75. A _____ is any object propelled through space by the applicationp of a force.
a. Thing
b. Projectile0
c. Undefined
d. Undefined

76. In mathematics, _____ are essentially word problems that are designed to use mathematical critical thinking in everyday situations.

Chapter 7. Factors, Divisors, and Factoring

a. Thing
c. Undefined
b. Application problems0
d. Undefined

77. _____ or arithmetics is the oldest and most elementary branch of mathematics, used by almost everyone, for tasks ranging from simple daily counting to advanced science and business calculations.

a. Thing
c. Undefined
b. Arithmetic0
d. Undefined

Chapter 8. Multiplication and Division of Rational Numbers and Expressions

1. The _____ of an algebraic expression is the same equation, but without parentheses.
   a. Expanded form0
   b. Thing
   c. Undefined
   d. Undefined

2. A _____ is a numeral used to indicate a count. The most common use of the word today is to name the part of a fraction that tells the number or count of equal parts.
   a. Numerator0
   b. Thing
   c. Undefined
   d. Undefined

3. A _____ is the part of a fraction that tells how many equal parts make up a whole, and which is used in the name of the fraction: "halves", "thirds", "fourths" or "quarters", "fifths" and so on.
   a. Denominator0
   b. Concept
   c. Undefined
   d. Undefined

4. In mathematics, a _____ number is a number which can be expressed as a ratio of two integers. Non-integer _____ numbers (commonly called fractions) are usually written as the vulgar fraction a / b, where b is not zero.
   a. Thing
   b. Rational0
   c. Undefined
   d. Undefined

5. The _____ are the only integral domain whose positive elements are well-ordered, and in which order is preserved by addition. Like the natural numbers, the _____ form a countably infinite set. The set of all _____ is usually denoted in mathematics by a boldface Z .
   a. Integers0
   b. Thing
   c. Undefined
   d. Undefined

6. An _____ is a combination of numbers, operators, grouping symbols and/or free variables and bound variables arranged in a meaningful way which can be evaluated..
   a. Expression0
   b. Thing
   c. Undefined
   d. Undefined

7. In mathematics, a _____ can mean either an element of the set {1, 2, 3, ...} (i.e the positive integers or the counting numbers) or an element of the set {0, 1, 2, 3, ...} (i.e. the non-negative integers).
   a. Natural number0
   b. Thing
   c. Undefined
   d. Undefined

8. In mathematics, a _____ can mean either an element of the set {1, 2, 3, ...} (i.e the positive integers) or an element of the set {0, 1, 2, 3, ...} (i.e. the non-negative integers).
   a. Concept
   b. Whole number0
   c. Undefined
   d. Undefined

9. _____ is a branch of mathematics concerning the study of structure, relation and quantity.
   a. Concept
   b. Algebra0
   c. Undefined
   d. Undefined

10. A _____ fraction is a fraction in which the absolute value of the numerator is less than the denominator--hence, the absolute value of the fraction is less than 1.

Chapter 8. Multiplication and Division of Rational Numbers and Expressions

a. Proper0
b. Thing
c. Undefined
d. Undefined

11. In mathematics, an inequality is a statement about the relative size or order of two objects. For example 14 > 10, or 14 is _____ 10.
   a. Greater than0
   b. Thing
   c. Undefined
   d. Undefined

12. A _____ is the sum of a whole number and a proper fraction.
   a. Thing
   b. Mixed number0
   c. Undefined
   d. Undefined

13. In Euclidean geometry, a _____ is the set of all points in a plane at a fixed distance, called the radius, from a given point, the center.
   a. Circle0
   b. Thing
   c. Undefined
   d. Undefined

14. In plane geometry, a _____ is a polygon with four equal sides, four right angles, and parallel opposite sides. In algebra, the _____ of a number is that number multiplied by itself.
   a. Thing
   b. Square0
   c. Undefined
   d. Undefined

15. In mathematics, _____ is an elementary arithmetic operation. When one of the numbers is a whole number, _____ is the repeated sum of the other number.
   a. Multiplication0
   b. Thing
   c. Undefined
   d. Undefined

16. The decimal separator is a symbol used to mark the boundary between the integral and the fractional parts of a decimal numeral. Terms implying the symbol used are _____ and decimal comma.
   a. Concept
   b. Decimal point0
   c. Undefined
   d. Undefined

17. The _____, the average in everyday English, which is also called the arithmetic _____ (and is distinguished from the geometric _____ or harmonic _____). The average is also called the sample _____. The expected value of a random variable, which is also called the population _____.
   a. Thing
   b. Mean0
   c. Undefined
   d. Undefined

18. A _____ is the part of the dividend that is left over when the dividend is not evenly divisible by the divisor.
   a. Remainder0
   b. Thing
   c. Undefined
   d. Undefined

19. In mathematics, a _____ of an integer n, also called a factor of n, is an integer which evenly divides n without leaving a remainder.

Chapter 8. Multiplication and Division of Rational Numbers and Expressions

  a. Thing
  c. Undefined
  b. Divisor0
  d. Undefined

20. _____ is a payment made by a company to its shareholders
  a. Dividend0
  c. Undefined
  b. Thing
  d. Undefined

21. In mathematics, a _____ is the end result of a division problem. It can also be expressed as the number of times the divisor divides into the dividend.
  a. Quotient0
  c. Undefined
  b. Thing
  d. Undefined

22. _____ is a kind of property which exists as magnitude or multitude. It is among the basic classes of things along with quality, substance, change, and relation.
  a. Amount0
  c. Undefined
  b. Thing
  d. Undefined

23. In mathematics, a _____ is a particular kind of polynomial, having just one term.
  a. Monomial0
  c. Undefined
  b. Thing
  d. Undefined

24. Equivalence is the condition of being _____ or essentially equal.
  a. Thing
  c. Undefined
  b. Equivalent0
  d. Undefined

25. In mathematics, a _____ is the result of multiplying, or an expression that identifies factors to be multiplied.
  a. Thing
  c. Undefined
  b. Product0
  d. Undefined

26. _____ is the largest positive integer that divides both numbers without remainder.
  a. Common Factor0
  c. Undefined
  b. Thing
  d. Undefined

27. In mathematics, factorization (British English: factorisation) or factoring is the decomposition of an object (for example, a number, a polynomial, or a matrix) into a product of other objects, or _____, which when multiplied together give the original.
  a. Factors0
  c. Undefined
  b. Thing
  d. Undefined

28. In mathematics, a _____ number (or a _____) is a natural number that has exactly two (distinct) natural number divisors, which are 1 and the _____ number itself.
  a. Prime0
  c. Undefined
  b. Thing
  d. Undefined

29. The _____ of a positive integer are the prime numbers that divide into that integer exactly, without leaving a remainder. The process of finding these numbers is called integer factorization, or prime factorization.

Chapter 8. Multiplication and Division of Rational Numbers and Expressions 83

    a. Thing
    c. Undefined
    b. Prime factor0
    d. Undefined

30. In mathematics, a _____ is an expression that is constructed from one or more variables and constants, using only the operations of addition, subtraction, multiplication, and constant positive whole number exponents. is a _____. Note in particular that division by an expression containing a variable is not in general allowed in polynomials. [1]
    a. Polynomial0
    c. Undefined
    b. Thing
    d. Undefined

31. _____ is a mathematical operation, written a^n, involving two numbers, the base a and the exponent n.
    a. Thing
    c. Undefined
    b. Exponentiating0
    d. Undefined

32. _____ is a mathematical operation, written a^n, involving two numbers, the base a and the exponent n.
    a. Exponentiation0
    c. Undefined
    b. Thing
    d. Undefined

33. A _____ is a symbolic representation denoting a quantity or expression. It often represents an "unknown" quantity that has the potential to change.
    a. Variable0
    c. Undefined
    b. Thing
    d. Undefined

34. The word _____ comes from the Latin word linearis, which means created by lines.
    a. Thing
    c. Undefined
    b. Linear0
    d. Undefined

35. A _____ is an equation in which each term is either a constant or the product of a constant times the first power of a variable.
    a. Linear equation0
    c. Undefined
    b. Thing
    d. Undefined

36. _____ the expected value of a random variable displays the average or central value of the variable. It is a summary value of the distribution of the variable.
    a. Determining0
    c. Undefined
    b. Thing
    d. Undefined

37. In mathematics, _____ refers to the rewriting of an expression into a simpler form.
    a. Thing
    c. Undefined
    b. Reduction0
    d. Undefined

38. In arithmetic and algebra, when a number or expression is both preceded and followed by a binary operation, an _____ is required for which operation should be applied first.
    a. Thing
    c. Undefined
    b. Order of operations0
    d. Undefined

39. A _____ is a polynomial function of the form $f(x) = ax^2 + bx + c$, where a, b, c are real numbers and a , 0.

Chapter 8. Multiplication and Division of Rational Numbers and Expressions

a. Event
b. Quadratic function0
c. Undefined
d. Undefined

40. In mathematics, a _____ is any function which can be written as the ratio of two polynomial functions.
a. Rational function0
b. Thing
c. Undefined
d. Undefined

41. The mathematical concept of a _____ expresses the intuitive idea of deterministic dependence between two quantities, one of which is viewed as primary and the other as secondary. A _____ then is a way to associate a unique output for each input of a specified type, for example, a real number or an element of a given set.
a. Thing
b. Function0
c. Undefined
d. Undefined

42. _____ has many meanings, most of which simply .
a. Thing
b. Power0
c. Undefined
d. Undefined

43. In mathematics, defined and _____ are used to explain whether or not expressions have meaningful, sensible, and unambiguous values.
a. Undefined0
b. Thing
c. Undefined
d. Undefined

44. _____ are objects, characters, or other concrete representations of ideas, concepts, or other abstractions.
a. Symbols0
b. Thing
c. Undefined
d. Undefined

45. In mathematics, a _____ is a constant multiplicative factor of a certain object. The object can be such things as a variable, a vector, a function, etc. For example, the _____ of $9x^2$ is 9.
a. Coefficient0
b. Thing
c. Undefined
d. Undefined

46. In mathematics, _____ are essentially word problems that are designed to use mathematical critical thinking in everyday situations.
a. Thing
b. Application problems0
c. Undefined
d. Undefined

47. A _____ is one of the basic shapes of geometry: a polygon with three vertices and three sides which are straight line segments.
a. Triangle0
b. Thing
c. Undefined
d. Undefined

48. In geometry, a _____ is defined as a quadrilateral where all four of its angles are right angles.
a. Thing
b. Rectangle0
c. Undefined
d. Undefined

Chapter 8. Multiplication and Division of Rational Numbers and Expressions

49. The metre (or _____, see spelling differences) is a measure of length. It is the basic unit of length in the metric system and in the International System of Units (SI), used around the world for general and scientific purposes.
   a. Meter0
   b. Concept
   c. Undefined
   d. Undefined

50. In the scientific method, an _____ (Latin: ex-+-periri, "of (or from) trying"), is a set of actions and observations, performed in the context of solving a particular problem or question, in order to support or falsify a hypothesis or research concerning phenomena.
   a. Experiment0
   b. Thing
   c. Undefined
   d. Undefined

51. A _____ is a quadrilateral, which is defined as a shape with four sides, which has a pair of parallel sides.
   a. Thing
   b. Trapezoid0
   c. Undefined
   d. Undefined

52. In mathematics, the _____ inverse of a number x, denoted $1/x$ or x^{-1}, is the number which, when multiplied by x, yields 1. The _____ inverse of x is also called the reciprocal of x.
   a. Thing
   b. Multiplicative0
   c. Undefined
   d. Undefined

53. _____ element of an element x with respect to a binary operation * with identity element e is an element y such that $x * y = y * x = e$. In particular,
   a. Thing
   b. Inverse0
   c. Undefined
   d. Undefined

54. U.S. liquid _____ is legally defined as 231 cubic inches, and is equal to 3.785411784 litres or abotu 0.13368 cubic feet. This is the most common definition of a _____. The U.S. fluid ounce is defined as 1/128 of a U.S. _____.
   a. Gallon0
   b. Thing
   c. Undefined
   d. Undefined

55. In mathematics, _____ is the decomposition of an object into a product of other objects, or factors, which when multiplied together give the original.
   a. Factoring0
   b. Thing
   c. Undefined
   d. Undefined

56. In arithmetic, _____ is a procedure for calculating the division of one integer, called the dividend, by another integer called the divisor, to produce a result called the quotient.
   a. Thing
   b. Long division0
   c. Undefined
   d. Undefined

57. A _____ is a negotiable instrument instructing a financial institution to pay a specific amount of a specific currency from a specific demand account held in the maker/depositor's name with that institution. Both the maker and payee may be natural persons or legal entities.

Chapter 8. Multiplication and Division of Rational Numbers and Expressions

    a. Check0
    b. Thing
    c. Undefined
    d. Undefined

58. _____ is a set, with some particular properties and usually some additional structure, such as the operations of addition or multiplication, for instance.
    a. Thing
    b. Space0
    c. Undefined
    d. Undefined

59. The _____ of measurement are a globally standardized and modernized form of the metric system.
    a. Units0
    b. Thing
    c. Undefined
    d. Undefined

60. A _____ is a one-dimensional picture in which the integers are shown as specially-marked points evenly spaced on a line.
    a. Number line0
    b. Thing
    c. Undefined
    d. Undefined

61. In mathematics, computing, linguistics, and related disciplines, an _____ is a finite list of well-defined instructions for accomplishing some task which, given an initial state, will terminate in a defined end-state.
    a. Concept
    b. Algorithm0
    c. Undefined
    d. Undefined

62. _____ is a numeral system in which each position is related to the next by a constant multiplier, a common ratio, called the base or radix of that numeral system.
    a. Thing
    b. Place value0
    c. Undefined
    d. Undefined

63. In mathematics, there are several meanings of _____ depending on the subject.
    a. Thing
    b. Degree0
    c. Undefined
    d. Undefined

64. _____ or arithmetics is the oldest and most elementary branch of mathematics, used by almost everyone, for tasks ranging from simple daily counting to advanced science and business calculations.
    a. Thing
    b. Arithmetic0
    c. Undefined
    d. Undefined

65. _____ is a mathematical subject that includes the study of limits, derivatives, integrals, and power series and constitutes a major part of modern university curriculum.
    a. Thing
    b. Calculus0
    c. Undefined
    d. Undefined

66. _____ is the chance that something is likely to happen or be the case.
    a. Probability0
    b. Thing
    c. Undefined
    d. Undefined

67. A _____ is a symbol or group of symbols, or a word in a natural language that represents a number.

a. Thing
b. Numeral 0
c. Undefined
d. Undefined

Chapter 9. Addition and Subtraction of Rational Numbers and Expressions

1. In mathematics, a _____ number is a number which can be expressed as a ratio of two integers. Non-integer _____ numbers (commonly called fractions) are usually written as the vulgar fraction a / b, where b is not zero.
   - a. Thing
   - b. Rational0
   - c. Undefined
   - d. Undefined

2. An _____ is a combination of numbers, operators, grouping symbols and/or free variables and bound variables arranged in a meaningful way which can be evaluated..
   - a. Thing
   - b. Expression0
   - c. Undefined
   - d. Undefined

3. A _____ is the part of a fraction that tells how many equal parts make up a whole, and which is used in the name of the fraction: "halves", "thirds", "fourths" or "quarters", "fifths" and so on.
   - a. Denominator0
   - b. Concept
   - c. Undefined
   - d. Undefined

4. A _____ is the sum of a whole number and a proper fraction.
   - a. Thing
   - b. Mixed number0
   - c. Undefined
   - d. Undefined

5. A _____ is a numeral used to indicate a count. The most common use of the word today is to name the part of a fraction that tells the number or count of equal parts.
   - a. Numerator0
   - b. Thing
   - c. Undefined
   - d. Undefined

6. _____ are objects, characters, or other concrete representations of ideas, concepts, or other abstractions.
   - a. Symbols0
   - b. Thing
   - c. Undefined
   - d. Undefined

7. Equivalence is the condition of being _____ or essentially equal.
   - a. Thing
   - b. Equivalent0
   - c. Undefined
   - d. Undefined

8. A _____ is the result of the addition of a set of numbers. The numbers may be natural numbers, complex numbers, matrices, or still more complicated objects. An infinite _____ is a subtle procedure known as a series.
   - a. Thing
   - b. Sum0
   - c. Undefined
   - d. Undefined

9. _____ is the largest positive integer that divides both numbers without remainder.
   - a. Common Factor0
   - b. Thing
   - c. Undefined
   - d. Undefined

10. In mathematics, factorization (British English: factorisation) or factoring is the decomposition of an object (for example, a number, a polynomial, or a matrix) into a product of other objects, or _____, which when multiplied together give the original.
    - a. Factors0
    - b. Thing
    - c. Undefined
    - d. Undefined

Chapter 9. Addition and Subtraction of Rational Numbers and Expressions

11. _____, either of the curved-bracket punctuation marks that together make a set of _____
    a. Thing
    b. Parentheses0
    c. Undefined
    d. Undefined

12. _____ is a mathematical operation, written a^n, involving two numbers, the base a and the exponent n.
    a. Exponentiating0
    b. Thing
    c. Undefined
    d. Undefined

13. _____ is a mathematical operation, written a^n, involving two numbers, the base a and the exponent n.
    a. Thing
    b. Exponentiation0
    c. Undefined
    d. Undefined

14. In mathematics, the _____ divisor of two non-zero integers, is the largest positive integer that divides both numbers without remainder.
    a. Greatest common0
    b. Thing
    c. Undefined
    d. Undefined

15. In Math the greates common divisor sometimes known as the _____ of two non- zero integers.
    a. Greatest common factor0
    b. Thing
    c. Undefined
    d. Undefined

16. The _____ are the only integral domain whose positive elements are well-ordered, and in which order is preserved by addition. Like the natural numbers, the _____ form a countably infinite set. The set of all _____ is usually denoted in mathematics by a boldface Z .
    a. Integers0
    b. Thing
    c. Undefined
    d. Undefined

17. In mathematics, the _____ of two non-zero integers, is the largest positive integer that divides both numbers without remainder.
    a. Thing
    b. Greatest common divisor0
    c. Undefined
    d. Undefined

18. A _____ of a number is the product of that number with any integer.
    a. Multiple0
    b. Thing
    c. Undefined
    d. Undefined

19. The _____ of two integers is the smallest positive integer that is a multiple of both intergers.
    a. Thing
    b. Least common multiple0
    c. Undefined
    d. Undefined

20. In mathematics, a _____ of an integer n, also called a factor of n, is an integer which evenly divides n without leaving a remainder.
    a. Divisor0
    b. Thing
    c. Undefined
    d. Undefined

21. In mathematics, a _____ is the result of multiplying, or an expression that identifies factors to be multiplied.

Chapter 9. Addition and Subtraction of Rational Numbers and Expressions

a. Product0
b. Thing
c. Undefined
d. Undefined

22. In mathematics, a _____ number (or a _____) is a natural number that has exactly two (distinct) natural number divisors, which are 1 and the _____ number itself.
a. Prime0
b. Thing
c. Undefined
d. Undefined

23. The _____ of a positive integer are the prime numbers that divide into that integer exactly, without leaving a remainder. The process of finding these numbers is called integer factorization, or prime factorization.
a. Thing
b. Prime factor0
c. Undefined
d. Undefined

24. In mathematics, _____ is the decomposition of an object into a product of other objects, or factors, which when multiplied together give the original.
a. Thing
b. Factoring0
c. Undefined
d. Undefined

25. _____, in number theory is the process of breaking down a composite number into smaller non-trivial divisors, which when multiplied together equal the original integer.
a. Integer factorization0
b. Thing
c. Undefined
d. Undefined

26. _____ is a natural number that has exactly two distinct natural number divisors, which are 1 and the _____ itself.
a. Prime number0
b. Thing
c. Undefined
d. Undefined

27. In mathematics, a _____ is a particular kind of polynomial, having just one term.
a. Thing
b. Monomial0
c. Undefined
d. Undefined

28. A _____ is a symbolic representation denoting a quantity or expression. It often represents an "unknown" quantity that has the potential to change.
a. Variable0
b. Thing
c. Undefined
d. Undefined

29. In mathematics, a _____ is an expression that is constructed from one or more variables and constants, using only the operations of addition, subtraction, multiplication, and constant positive whole number exponents. is a _____. Note in particular that division by an expression containing a variable is not in general allowed in polynomials. [1]
a. Polynomial0
b. Thing
c. Undefined
d. Undefined

30. In mathematics, a _____ is a constant multiplicative factor of a certain object. The object can be such things as a variable, a vector, a function, etc. For example, the _____ of $9x^2$ is 9.

Chapter 9. Addition and Subtraction of Rational Numbers and Expressions

a. Coefficient0
b. Thing
c. Undefined
d. Undefined

31. In geometry, a _____ is defined as a quadrilateral where all four of its angles are right angles.
    a. Rectangle0
    b. Thing
    c. Undefined
    d. Undefined

32. In mathematics, _____ is an elementary arithmetic operation. When one of the numbers is a whole number, _____ is the repeated sum of the other number.
    a. Multiplication0
    b. Thing
    c. Undefined
    d. Undefined

33. A _____ is a negotiable instrument instructing a financial institution to pay a specific amount of a specific currency from a specific demand account held in the maker/depositor's name with that institution. Both the maker and payee may be natural persons or legal entities.
    a. Thing
    b. Check0
    c. Undefined
    d. Undefined

34. In mathematics, a _____ can mean either an element of the set {1, 2, 3, ...} (i.e the positive integers or the counting numbers) or an element of the set {0, 1, 2, 3, ...} (i.e. the non-negative integers).
    a. Natural number0
    b. Thing
    c. Undefined
    d. Undefined

35. _____ has many meanings, most of which simply .
    a. Thing
    b. Power0
    c. Undefined
    d. Undefined

36. In elementary algebra, a _____ is a polynomial with two terms: the sum of two monomials. It is the simplest kind of polynomial except for a monomial.
    a. Thing
    b. Binomial0
    c. Undefined
    d. Undefined

37. In mathematics, a _____ can mean either an element of the set {1, 2, 3, ...} (i.e the positive integers) or an element of the set {0, 1, 2, 3, ...} (i.e. the non-negative integers).
    a. Concept
    b. Whole number0
    c. Undefined
    d. Undefined

38. Regrouping is the act of putting ones into groups of 10. For example, the 1 on the far right of 131 would be denoted _____ if the digit of the number being subtracted is larger than 1, such as 131-99.
    a. Thing
    b. By 100
    c. Undefined
    d. Undefined

39. A _____ is a unit of length, usually used to measure distance, in a number of different systems, including Imperial units, United States customary units and Norwegian/Swedish mil. Its size can vary from system to system, but in each is between 1 and 10 kilometers. In contemporary English contexts _____ refers to either:

Chapter 9. Addition and Subtraction of Rational Numbers and Expressions

a. Thing
b. Mile0
c. Undefined
d. Undefined

40. The _____, the average in everyday English, which is also called the arithmetic _____ (and is distinguished from the geometric _____ or harmonic _____). The average is also called the sample _____. The expected value of a random variable, which is also called the population _____.
   a. Thing
   b. Mean0
   c. Undefined
   d. Undefined

41. In mathematics, _____ expressions is used to reduce the expression into the lowest possible term.
   a. Thing
   b. Simplifying0
   c. Undefined
   d. Undefined

42. Two mathematical objects are equal if and only if they are precisely the same in every way. This defines a binary relation, _____, denoted by the sign of _____ "=" in such a way that the statement "x = y" means that x and y are equal.
   a. Equality0
   b. Thing
   c. Undefined
   d. Undefined

43. _____ variables are variables other than the independent variable that may bear any effect on the behavior of the subject being studied.
   a. Thing
   b. Extraneous0
   c. Undefined
   d. Undefined

44. _____ means in succession or back-to-back
   a. Thing
   b. Consecutive0
   c. Undefined
   d. Undefined

45. In mathematics, _____ are essentially word problems that are designed to use mathematical critical thinking in everyday situations.
   a. Application problems0
   b. Thing
   c. Undefined
   d. Undefined

46. In mathematics, the multiplicative inverse of a number x, denoted 1/x or x^{-1}, is the number which, when multiplied by x, yields 1. The multiplicative inverse of x is also called the _____ of x.
   a. Reciprocal0
   b. Thing
   c. Undefined
   d. Undefined

47. A _____ is a special kind of ratio, indicating a relationship between two measurements with different units, such as miles to gallons or cents to pounds.
   a. Thing
   b. Rate0
   c. Undefined
   d. Undefined

48. _____ is a kind of property which exists as magnitude or multitude. It is among the basic classes of things along with quality, substance, change, and relation.

Chapter 9. Addition and Subtraction of Rational Numbers and Expressions

    a. Amount0   b. Thing
    c. Undefined   d. Undefined

49. _____ is the transport of people on a trip/journey or the process or time involved in a person or object moving from one location to another.
    a. Travel0
    b. Thing
    c. Undefined
    d. Undefined

50. _____ is a unit of speed, expressing the number of international miles covered per hour.
    a. Thing
    b. Miles per hour0
    c. Undefined
    d. Undefined

51. In mathematics, a matrix can be thought of as each row or _____ being a vector. Hence, a space formed by row vectors or _____ vectors are said to be a row space or a _____ space.
    a. Concept
    b. Column0
    c. Undefined
    d. Undefined

52. In mathematics, a _____ is a two-dimensional manifold or surface that is perfectly flat.
    a. Thing
    b. Plane0
    c. Undefined
    d. Undefined

53. In mathematics, an _____, mean, or central tendency of a data set refers to a measure of the "middle" or "expected" value of the data set.
    a. Concept
    b. Average0
    c. Undefined
    d. Undefined

54. _____ are a measure of time.
    a. Minutes0
    b. Thing
    c. Undefined
    d. Undefined

55. In botany, _____ are above-ground plant organs specialized for photosynthesis. Their characteristics are typically analyzed by using Fiobonacci's sequences.
    a. Thing
    b. Leaves0
    c. Undefined
    d. Undefined

56. _____ is the largest city in the state of Texas and the fourth-largest in the United States. As of the 2005 U.S. Census estimate, it had a population of more than 2 million.
    a. Thing
    b. Houston0
    c. Undefined
    d. Undefined

57. _____ is a state located in the southern and southwestern regions of the United States of America.
    a. Thing
    b. Texas0
    c. Undefined
    d. Undefined

58. In mathematics, a _____ or rhodonea curve is a sinusoid plotted in polar coordinates.

Chapter 9. Addition and Subtraction of Rational Numbers and Expressions

    a. Thing
    c. Undefined
    b. Rose0
    d. Undefined

59. A _____ is one of the basic shapes of geometry: a polygon with three vertices and three sides which are straight line segments.
    a. Thing
    c. Undefined
    b. Triangle0
    d. Undefined

60. _____ is the distance around a given two-dimensional object. As a general rule, the _____ of a polygon can always be calculated by adding all the length of the sides together. So, the formula for triangles is P = a + b + c, where a, b and c stand for each side of it. For quadrilaterals the equation is P = a + b + c + d. For equilateral polygons, P = na, where n is the number of sides and a is the side length.
    a. Thing
    c. Undefined
    b. Perimeter0
    d. Undefined

61. The metre (or _____, see spelling differences) is a measure of length. It is the basic unit of length in the metric system and in the International System of Units (SI), used around the world for general and scientific purposes.
    a. Meter0
    c. Undefined
    b. Concept
    d. Undefined

62. A _____ is a unit of length in the metric system, equal to one thousand metres, the current SI base unit of length
    a. Thing
    c. Undefined
    b. Kilometer0
    d. Undefined

63. The State of _____ is a state located in the Rocky Mountain region of the United States of America.
    a. Thing
    c. Undefined
    b. Colorado0
    d. Undefined

64. A _____ is a quantity that denotes the proportional amount or magnitude of one quantity relative to another.
    a. Thing
    c. Undefined
    b. Ratio0
    d. Undefined

65. _____ is a branch of mathematics which deals with triangles, particularly triangles in a plane where one angle of the triangle is 90 degrees, and a variety of other topological relations such as spheres, in other branches, such as spherical _____.
    a. Thing
    c. Undefined
    b. Trigonometry0
    d. Undefined

66. _____ or arithmetics is the oldest and most elementary branch of mathematics, used by almost everyone, for tasks ranging from simple daily counting to advanced science and business calculations.
    a. Arithmetic0
    c. Undefined
    b. Thing
    d. Undefined

67. _____ is a branch of mathematics concerning the study of structure, relation and quantity.

Chapter 9. Addition and Subtraction of Rational Numbers and Expressions

a. Concept
b. Algebra0
c. Undefined
d. Undefined

68. _____ is a mathematical subject that includes the study of limits, derivatives, integrals, and power series and constitutes a major part of modern university curriculum.
   a. Thing
   b. Calculus0
   c. Undefined
   d. Undefined

69. _____, from Latin meaning "to make progress", is defined in two different ways. Pure economic _____ is the increase in wealth that an investor has from making an investment, taking into consideration all costs associated with that investment including the opportunity cost of capital.
   a. Profit0
   b. Thing
   c. Undefined
   d. Undefined

70. _____ is a way of expressing a number as a fraction of 100 per cent meaning "per hundred".
   a. Thing
   b. Percent0
   c. Undefined
   d. Undefined

71. _____ is a business term for the amount of money that a company receives from its activities in a given period, mostly from sales of products and/or services to customers
   a. Revenue0
   b. Thing
   c. Undefined
   d. Undefined

72. _____ is the fee paid on borrowed money.
   a. Interest0
   b. Thing
   c. Undefined
   d. Undefined

Chapter 10. Ratios, Percents, and Applications

1. A _____ is the relationship between two quantities. It is expressed as the quotient of two numbers, or as two numbers separated by a colon (pronounced "to"). A number that can be written as a _____ of two integers is a rational number.
   - a. -equivalence
   - b. Ratio10
   - c. Undefined
   - d. Undefined

2. _____ is the result of assigning numbers to objects to abstractly represent the objects or characteristics of the objects.
   - a. Measurement10
   - b. -equivalence
   - c. Undefined
   - d. Undefined

3. Another word for independent variables in the analysis of variance is _____.
   - a. Factors10
   - b. -equivalence
   - c. Undefined
   - d. Undefined

4. _____ consist of the positive natural numbers (1, 2, 3, ...), their negatives (−1, −2, −3, ...) and the number zero.
   - a. ADE classification
   - b. Integers10
   - c. Undefined
   - d. Undefined

5. When the parts of a fraction have no common factors, the fraction is said to be <U>reduced</U> to lowest terms.
   - a. Reduced10
   - b. -equivalence
   - c. Undefined
   - d. Undefined

6. _____ is used synonymously for variable.
   - a. Factor10
   - b. -equivalence
   - c. Undefined
   - d. Undefined

7. A _____ number is a natural number greater than one that is only divisible by one and itself.
   - a. -equivalence
   - b. Prime10
   - c. Undefined
   - d. Undefined

8. A _____ is a positive integer (1,2,3,...).
   - a. -equivalence
   - b. Natural number10
   - c. Undefined
   - d. Undefined

9. <U>Multiplication</U> is a quick way of adding identical numbers. For example, the sum 7 + 7 + 7 can be found by multiplying 3 times 7. This model is reflected in the use of the word times as a synonym for multiplied by. The resuult of multiplying numbers is called a product. The numbers being multiplied are called factors.
   - a. Multiplication10
   - b. -equivalence
   - c. Undefined
   - d. Undefined

10. The bottom part of any fraction represents the number of pieces in one whole unit. This bottom part is called the <U>denominator.</U>
    - a. Denominator10
    - b. -equivalence
    - c. Undefined
    - d. Undefined

Chapter 10. Ratios, Percents, and Applications

11. The top part of the fraction is called the <U>numerator</U>. It could also be called the dividend, but _____ is preferred.
    a. Numerator10
    b. -equivalence
    c. Undefined
    d. Undefined

12. _____, or less commonly, denary, usually refers to the base 10 numeral system.
    a. -equivalence
    b. Decimal10
    c. Undefined
    d. Undefined

13. A _____ is a quotient of numbers, like 3⁄4, or more generally, an element of a quotient field.
    a. Fraction10
    b. -equivalence
    c. Undefined
    d. Undefined

14. An <U>equation</U> is represented by two expressions that have the same value.
    a. Equation10
    b. ADE classification
    c. Undefined
    d. Undefined

15. _____ are characteristics or properties of an object that can take on one or more different values.
    a. Variables10
    b. -equivalence
    c. Undefined
    d. Undefined

16. The number of times a particular score or event occurs with respect to the total number of events or scores is called its _____.
    a. Proportion10
    b. -equivalence
    c. Undefined
    d. Undefined

17. A <U>quadratic</U> contains at least one squared term.
    a. Quadratic10
    b. -equivalence
    c. Undefined
    d. Undefined

18. A _____ is an equation which is constructed by equating two linear functions of which the highest exponent is one.
    a. -equivalence
    b. Linear equation10
    c. Undefined
    d. Undefined

19. A _____ is a well-defined collection of objects considered as a whole.
    a. Set10
    b. -equivalence
    c. Undefined
    d. Undefined

20. An _____ is an indication of the value of an unknown quantity based on observed data. More formally, an _____ is the particular value of an estimator that is obtained from a particular sample of data and used to indicate the value of a parameter.
    a. Estimate10
    b. ADE classification
    c. Undefined
    d. Undefined

Chapter 10. Ratios, Percents, and Applications

21. A _____ is a subset or portion of a population. Samples are extremely important in the field of statistical analysis, since due to economic and practical constraints we usually cannot make measurements on every single member of the particular population.
   a. Sample10
   b. -equivalence
   c. Undefined
   d. Undefined

22. _____ is the study of quantity, structure, space, and change. Historically, _____ developed from counting, calculation, measurement, and the study of the shapes and motions of physical objects, through the use of abstraction and deductive reasoning.
   a. Mathematics10
   b. -equivalence
   c. Undefined
   d. Undefined

23. A percentage is a way of expressing a proportion, a ratio or a fraction as a whole number, by using 100 as the denominator. A number such as "45%" ("45 percent" or "45 per cent") is shorthand for the fraction 45/100 or 0.45.As an illustration,"45 _____ of human beings..." is equivalent to both of the following:"45 out of every 100 people..." "0.45 of the human population..." One way to think about percentages is to realize that "one percent", represented by the symbol %, is simply the number 1/100, or 0.01.
   a. Percent10
   b. -equivalence
   c. Undefined
   d. Undefined

24. _____ demonstrates that when equal quantities are multiplied by equal quantities their products are equal.
   a. Multiplication property of equality10
   b. -equivalence
   c. Undefined
   d. Undefined

25. The very fact that we are measuring objects with respect to some characteristic implies that the objects differ in that characteristic; or stated in another way, that the characteristic can take on a number of different values. These properties or characteristics of an object that can assume two or more different values are referred to as a _____.
   a. -equivalence
   b. Variable10
   c. Undefined
   d. Undefined

26. _____ or arithmetics (from the Greek word áñéèìüò = number) in common usage is a branch of (or the forerunner of) mathematics which records elementary properties of certain operations on numerals, though in usage by professional mathematicians, it often is treated as a synonym for number theory.
   a. ADE classification
   b. Arithmetic10
   c. Undefined
   d. Undefined

27. An _____ combines numbers, operators, and/or variables but contains no equal or inequality sign.
   a. ADE classification
   b. Expression10
   c. Undefined
   d. Undefined

28. _____ (or summation) is one of the basic operations of arithmetic. In its simplest form, _____ combines two numbers, the augend and addend, into a single number, the sum.
   a. ADE classification
   b. Addition10
   c. Undefined
   d. Undefined

Chapter 10. Ratios, Percents, and Applications

29. A number that is raised to a power, or _____ of an exponential function. This finds common use, for example, in the depiction of numbers, for instance, 10 is the _____ used in the decimal system, whereas 2 is the _____ in the binary numeral system.
   a. -equivalence
   b. Base10
   c. Undefined
   d. Undefined

30. a <U>rational number </U>(or informally fraction) is a ratio or quotient of two integers, usually written as the fraction a/b, where b is not zero. Each _____ can be written in infinitely many forms, for example 3 / 6 = 2 / 4 = 1 / 2. When rational numbers are turned into the decimal equivalents the numbers eventually end or repeat.
   a. Rational number10
   b. -equivalence
   c. Undefined
   d. Undefined

Chapter 11. Roots and Radicals

1. _____ (or summation) is one of the basic operations of arithmetic. In its simplest form, _____ combines two numbers, the augend and addend, into a single number, the sum.
   a. Addition11
   b. ADE classification
   c. Undefined
   d. Undefined

2. _____ is one of the four basic arithmetic operations. It is usually denoted by an infix minus sign. The traditional names for the terms of the _____ in the formulac − b = a are minuend (c) − subtrahend (b) = difference (a).
   a. -equivalence
   b. Subtraction11
   c. Undefined
   d. Undefined

3. Addition (or summation) is one of the basic operations of arithmetic. In its simplest form, addition combines two numbers, the augend and addend, into a single number, the _____. Adding more numbers can be viewed as repeated addition. (Repeated addition of the number one is the most basic form of counting.) By extension, the addition of zero numbers, one number, or infinitely many numbers can be defined.
   a. Sum11
   b. -equivalence
   c. Undefined
   d. Undefined

4. <U>Multiplication</U> is a quick way of adding identical numbers. For example, the sum 7 + 7 + 7 can be found by multiplying 3 times 7. This model is reflected in the use of the word times as a synonym for multiplied by. The resuult of multiplying numbers is called a product. The numbers being multiplied are called factors.
   a. Multiplication11
   b. -equivalence
   c. Undefined
   d. Undefined

5. A quadrilateral with 4 equal sides and all right angles is called a <U>square.</U>
   a. Square11
   b. -equivalence
   c. Undefined
   d. Undefined

6. When a given number is the product of another number by itself, the another number is called the <U>square root</U>. Ex: 25 = 5 x 5 so 5 is the _____ of 25.
   a. Square root11
   b. -equivalence
   c. Undefined
   d. Undefined

7. The probability of correctly rejecting a false Ho is referred to as _____.
   a. -equivalence
   b. Power11
   c. Undefined
   d. Undefined

8. An _____ combines numbers, operators, and/or variables but contains no equal or inequality sign.
   a. ADE classification
   b. Expression11
   c. Undefined
   d. Undefined

9. _____ refers to taking a root of a number. _____ 16 means to find the square root of 16, which is 4.
   a. Radical11
   b. -equivalence
   c. Undefined
   d. Undefined

10. The _____ is the term under the radical sign.

Chapter 11. Roots and Radicals

    a. Radicand11   b. -equivalence
    c. Undefined   d. Undefined

11. _____, or less commonly, denary, usually refers to the base 10 numeral system.
    a. Decimal11   b. -equivalence
    c. Undefined   d. Undefined

12. a <U>rational number </U>(or informally fraction) is a ratio or quotient of two integers, usually written as the fraction a/b, where b is not zero. Each _____ can be written in infinitely many forms, for example 3 / 6 = 2 / 4 = 1 / 2. When rational numbers are turned into the decimal equivalents the numbers eventually end or repeat.
    a. Rational number11   b. -equivalence
    c. Undefined   d. Undefined

13. When two of the same number are multiplied, the result is called a <U>perfect square</U>.
    a. -equivalence   b. Perfect square11
    c. Undefined   d. Undefined

14. An irrational number is any real number that is not a rational number, i.e., one that cannot be written as a ratio of two integers, i.e., it is not of the forma/b where a and b are integers and b is not zero. It can readily be shown that the _____ are precisely those numbers whose expansion in any given base (decimal, binary, etc) never ends and never enters a periodic pattern, but no mathematician takes that to be a definition. Almost all real numbers are irrational, in a sense which is defined more precisely below.Some _____ are algebraic numbers, such as ã2, the square root of two, and 3 ã5, the cube root of 5; others are transcendental numbers such as ƒÎ and e.
    a. ADE classification   b. Irrational numbers11
    c. Undefined   d. Undefined

15. _____ are characteristics or properties of an object that can take on one or more different values.
    a. Variables11   b. -equivalence
    c. Undefined   d. Undefined

16. One number is <U>divisible by </U>another number if division is completed without a remainder. Since 8 is _____ 2, we say 8 is _____ 2.
    a. Divisible by11   b. -equivalence
    c. Undefined   d. Undefined

17. The <U>exponent </U>indicates how many of the base to multiply together to get the product. When 5 to the third power is 125, then 3 is the _____ and can also be called a power.
    a. ADE classification   b. Exponent11
    c. Undefined   d. Undefined

18. The very fact that we are measuring objects with respect to some characteristic implies that the objects differ in that characteristic; or stated in another way, that the characteristic can take on a number of different values. These properties or characteristics of an object that can assume two or more different values are referred to as a _____.
    a. -equivalence   b. Variable11
    c. Undefined   d. Undefined

Chapter 11. Roots and Radicals

19. _____ is the study of quantity, structure, space, and change. Historically, _____ developed from counting, calculation, measurement, and the study of the shapes and motions of physical objects, through the use of abstraction and deductive reasoning.
   a. -equivalence
   b. Mathematics11
   c. Undefined
   d. Undefined

20. When the parts of a fraction have no common factors, the fraction is said to be <U>reduced</U> to lowest terms.
   a. Reduced11
   b. -equivalence
   c. Undefined
   d. Undefined

21. A _____ is an undefined term. However, it is often thought of as a series of points. A _____ has one dimension - length. A _____ is either named by a lower case letter or by two points on the _____.
   a. Line11
   b. -equivalence
   c. Undefined
   d. Undefined

22. Another word for independent variables in the analysis of variance is _____.
   a. -equivalence
   b. Factors11
   c. Undefined
   d. Undefined

23. _____ is used synonymously for variable.
   a. -equivalence
   b. Factor11
   c. Undefined
   d. Undefined

24. A _____ number is a natural number greater than one that is only divisible by one and itself.
   a. -equivalence
   b. Prime11
   c. Undefined
   d. Undefined

25. A _____ is the result of multiplying, or an expression that identifies factors to be multiplied
   a. -equivalence
   b. Product11
   c. Undefined
   d. Undefined

26. <U>Twice</U> means to multiply by 2.
   a. Twice11
   b. -equivalence
   c. Undefined
   d. Undefined

27. In order to determine when to find a square root a special symbol called the <U>radical sign</U>. It looks like a check mark was added to the front of the division symbol.
   a. Radical sign11
   b. -equivalence
   c. Undefined
   d. Undefined

28. A<U> _____ </U>is a collection of the addition and multipication of terms so that at least one term contains a variable.
   a. Variable expression11
   b. -equivalence
   c. Undefined
   d. Undefined

Chapter 11. Roots and Radicals

29. _____ are intuitively defined as numbers that are in one-to-one correspondence with the points on an infinite line—the number line. The term "real number" is a retronym coined in response to "imaginary number" _____ may be rational or irrational; algebraic or transcendental; and positive, negative, or zero _____ measure continuous quantities. They may in theory be expressed by decimal fractions that have an infinite sequence of digits to the right of the decimal point; these are often (mis-)represented in the same form as 324.823211247... (where the three dots express that there would still be more digits to come, no matter how many more might be added at the end).
   a. -equivalence
   b. Real numbers11
   c. Undefined
   d. Undefined

30. The bottom part of any fraction represents the number of pieces in one whole unit. This bottom part is called the <U>denominator.</U>
   a. -equivalence
   b. Denominator11
   c. Undefined
   d. Undefined

31. The top part of the fraction is called the <U>numerator</U>. It could also be called the dividend, but _____ is preferred.
   a. Numerator11
   b. -equivalence
   c. Undefined
   d. Undefined

32. A _____ is a multiplicative factor of a certain object such as a variable (for example, the coefficients of a polynomial), a basis vector, a basis function and so on. Usually, the objects and the coefficients are indexed in the same way, leading to expressions such as $a_1 x_1 + a_2 x_2 + a_3 x_3 + ...$ where a_n is the _____ of the variable x_n for each n = 1, 2, 3, ...
   a. -equivalence
   b. Coefficient11
   c. Undefined
   d. Undefined

33. _____ is the property of multiplication over addition which demonstrates that for all numbers a,b,c; a(b+c)=ab+ac, and ab+ac=a(b+c).
   a. Distributive property11
   b. -equivalence
   c. Undefined
   d. Undefined

34. _____ occur when each term contains the very same variable to the same power. 3x and -5x are examples of _____.
   a. Like terms11
   b. -equivalence
   c. Undefined
   d. Undefined

35. It is necessary that everyone using mathematics do the operations in the same order so that the same problem will give the same answer for everyone doing this propblem. To do this, the <U>order of operations</U> were made..
   a. ADE classification
   b. Order of operations11
   c. Undefined
   d. Undefined

36. A _____ is the end result of a division problem. For example, in the problem 6 ÷ 3, the _____ would be 2, while 6 would be called the dividend, and 3 the divisor
   a. Quotient11
   b. -equivalence
   c. Undefined
   d. Undefined

Chapter 11. Roots and Radicals

37. The same statistical principles apply to the evaluation of observed _____ between sets of data. The field of statistics provides the necessary techniques for making statements of our certainty that there are real as opposed to chance _____.
   a. -equivalence
   b. Differences11
   c. Undefined
   d. Undefined

38. A <U>quadratic</U> contains at least one squared term.
   a. Quadratic11
   b. -equivalence
   c. Undefined
   d. Undefined

39. A _____ is a quotient of numbers, like 3⁄4, or more generally, an element of a quotient field.
   a. Fraction11
   b. -equivalence
   c. Undefined
   d. Undefined

40. An <U>equation</U> is represented by two expressions that have the same value.
   a. ADE classification
   b. Equation11
   c. Undefined
   d. Undefined

41. A number that does not change in value in a given situation is a _____.
   a. Constant11
   b. -equivalence
   c. Undefined
   d. Undefined

42. A <U>right triangle </U>must contain a right angle.
   a. -equivalence
   b. Right triangle11
   c. Undefined
   d. Undefined

43. Any polygon that has 3 sides is called a <U>triangle</U>.
   a. -equivalence
   b. Triangle11
   c. Undefined
   d. Undefined

44. An <U>angle</U> is composed of two rays that have a common endpoint, called the vertex. Each _____ is named by a lower case letter or by one point from each ray and the vertex inbetween. _____ a might be the same _____ as _____ ABC.
   a. Angle11
   b. ADE classification
   c. Undefined
   d. Undefined

45. A <U>hypotenuse </U>occurs in a right triangle and is the side opposite the right angle. It will also be the longest side of a right triangle.
   a. Hypotenuse11
   b. -equivalence
   c. Undefined
   d. Undefined

46. The <U>opposite </U>of a number is the number that makes a sum zero. In most cases, this means just to change the sign. 3 is the _____ of -3.
   a. ADE classification
   b. Opposite11
   c. Undefined
   d. Undefined

Chapter 11. Roots and Radicals

47. Any angle that equals 90 degrees is called a <U>right angle</U>. This angle also forms perpendicular lines.
    a. -equivalence
    b. Right angle11
    c. Undefined
    d. Undefined

48. A quadrilateral with opposite sides equal and parallel and containing all right angles is called a <U>rectangle.</U>
    a. Rectangle11
    b. -equivalence
    c. Undefined
    d. Undefined

49. A <U>point </U>is an undefined term. We usually represent this by a dot, but a _____ actually has no dimension. A capital letter names any _____.
    a. Point11
    b. -equivalence
    c. Undefined
    d. Undefined

50. When a number in decimal form does not repeat nor terminate, it is an <U>irrational number</U>. Pi and the square root of 7 are example s of an _____.
    a. Irrational number11
    b. ADE classification
    c. Undefined
    d. Undefined

51. A number that is raised to a power, or _____ of an exponential function. This finds common use, for example, in the depiction of numbers, for instance, 10 is the _____ used in the decimal system, whereas 2 is the _____ in the binary numeral system.
    a. -equivalence
    b. Base11
    c. Undefined
    d. Undefined

52. A _____ is simply a polynomial with two terms such as this example: 2x + 7.
    a. -equivalence
    b. Binomial11
    c. Undefined
    d. Undefined

53. A _____ is simply a polynomial with three terms connect by addition and multiplication.
    a. Trinomial11
    b. -equivalence
    c. Undefined
    d. Undefined

Chapter 12. Solving Quadratic Equations

1. _____ consist of the positive natural numbers (1, 2, 3, ...), their negatives (−1, −2, −3, ...) and the number zero.
   a. ADE classification
   b. Integers12
   c. Undefined
   d. Undefined

2. A <U>quadratic</U> contains at least one squared term.
   a. -equivalence
   b. Quadratic12
   c. Undefined
   d. Undefined

3. _____ is used synonymously for variable.
   a. Factor12
   b. -equivalence
   c. Undefined
   d. Undefined

4. A _____ is a well-defined collection of objects considered as a whole.
   a. -equivalence
   b. Set12
   c. Undefined
   d. Undefined

5. A quadrilateral with 4 equal sides and all right angles is called a <U>square.</U>
   a. Square12
   b. -equivalence
   c. Undefined
   d. Undefined

6. _____ are intuitively defined as numbers that are in one-to-one correspondence with the points on an infinite line—the number line. The term "real number" is a retronym coined in response to "imaginary number" _____ may be rational or irrational; algebraic or transcendental; and positive, negative, or zero _____ measure continuous quantities. They may in theory be expressed by decimal fractions that have an infinite sequence of digits to the right of the decimal point; these are often (mis-)represented in the same form as 324.823211247... (where the three dots express that there would still be more digits to come, no matter how many more might be added at the end).
   a. Real numbers12
   b. -equivalence
   c. Undefined
   d. Undefined

7. An <U>equation</U> is represented by two expressions that have the same value.
   a. ADE classification
   b. Equation12
   c. Undefined
   d. Undefined

8. A _____ is the end result of a division problem. For example, in the problem 6 ÷ 3, the _____ would be 2, while 6 would be called the dividend, and 3 the divisor
   a. -equivalence
   b. Quotient12
   c. Undefined
   d. Undefined

9. A _____ is the result of multiplying, or an expression that identifies factors to be multiplied
   a. Product12
   b. -equivalence
   c. Undefined
   d. Undefined

10. When a given number is the product of another number by itself, the another number is called the <U>square root</U>. Ex: 25 = 5 x 5 so 5 is the _____ of 25.
    a. Square root12
    b. -equivalence
    c. Undefined
    d. Undefined

Chapter 12. Solving Quadratic Equations

11. Addition (or summation) is one of the basic operations of arithmetic. In its simplest form, addition combines two numbers, the augend and addend, into a single number, the _____. Adding more numbers can be viewed as repeated addition. (Repeated addition of the number one is the most basic form of counting.) By extension, the addition of zero numbers, one number, or infinitely many numbers can be defined.
    a. Sum12
    b. -equivalence
    c. Undefined
    d. Undefined

12. When two of the same number are multiplied, the result is called a <U>perfect square</U>.
    a. Perfect square12
    b. -equivalence
    c. Undefined
    d. Undefined

13. A _____ is a class of simple functions where they are constructed using only multiplication and addition of terms.
    a. -equivalence
    b. Polynomial12
    c. Undefined
    d. Undefined

14. A _____ is simply a polynomial with three terms connect by addition and multiplication.
    a. Trinomial12
    b. -equivalence
    c. Undefined
    d. Undefined

15. A _____ is simply a polynomial with two terms such as this example: 2x + 7.
    a. Binomial12
    b. -equivalence
    c. Undefined
    d. Undefined

16. factorization or _____ is the decomposition of an object (for example, a number, a polynomial, or a matrix) into a product of other objects, or factors, which when multiplied together give the original. For example, the number 15 factors into primes as 3 × 5; and the polynomial x2 − 4 factors as (x − 2)(x + 2). In both cases, we obtain a product of simpler things.
    a. -equivalence
    b. Factoring12
    c. Undefined
    d. Undefined

17. A <U>quadratic equation </U>is written in standard form as ax^3+ bx + c = 0. In general, a _____ must contain a squared term.
    a. -equivalence
    b. Quadratic equation12
    c. Undefined
    d. Undefined

18. A _____ is a quotient of numbers, like 3⁄4, or more generally, an element of a quotient field.
    a. -equivalence
    b. Fraction12
    c. Undefined
    d. Undefined

19. A quadrilateral with opposite sides equal and parallel and containing all right angles is called a <U>rectangle.</U>
    a. Rectangle12
    b. -equivalence
    c. Undefined
    d. Undefined

20. A _____ is a concrete example of an item or a specification against which all others may be measured. For example, there are "primary standards" for length, mass (see Kilogram standard), and other units of measure, kept by laboratories and standards organizations.

Chapter 12. Solving Quadratic Equations

    a. Standard12
    c. Undefined
    b. -equivalence
    d. Undefined

21. <U>FOIL</U> is a way to multiply two binomials. The letters stand for: F for multiplying the FIRST terms, the O for multiplying OUTSIDE terms, the I for multiplying the INSIDE terms, and the L for multiplying the LAST terms.
    a. FOIL12
    c. Undefined
    b. -equivalence
    d. Undefined

22. _____ refers to taking a root of a number. _____ 16 means to find the square root of 16, which is 4.
    a. Radical12
    c. Undefined
    b. -equivalence
    d. Undefined

23. A _____ is an equation which is constructed by equating two linear functions of which the highest exponent is one.
    a. -equivalence
    c. Undefined
    b. Linear equation12
    d. Undefined

24. Any time one number is on the left side of another number on a number line, the first number is <U>less than </U>the second number. The symbol for this is <.
    a. Less than12
    c. Undefined
    b. -equivalence
    d. Undefined

25. The _____ or central tendency of a list of n numbers. All the values are added together and then divided by the number of values. It is also call the mean..
    a. ADE classification
    c. Undefined
    b. Average12
    d. Undefined

26. _____ is the change in x between two points
    a. -equivalence
    c. Undefined
    b. Run12
    d. Undefined

27. The answer to subtraction is called the <U>difference</U>.
    a. -equivalence
    c. Undefined
    b. Difference12
    d. Undefined

28. <U>Twice</U> means to multiply by 2.
    a. -equivalence
    c. Undefined
    b. Twice12
    d. Undefined

29. A <U>point </U>is an undefined term. We usually represent this by a dot, but a _____ actually has no dimension. A capital letter names any _____.
    a. Point12
    c. Undefined
    b. -equivalence
    d. Undefined

30. A _____ is a number or variable, or the product or quotient of a number or variable.

Chapter 12. Solving Quadratic Equations

a. -equivalence
c. Undefined
b. Term12
d. Undefined

31. The same statistical principles apply to the evaluation of observed _____ between sets of data. The field of statistics provides the necessary techniques for making statements of our certainty that there are real as opposed to chance _____.
  a. -equivalence
  b. Differences12
  c. Undefined
  d. Undefined

32. The very fact that we are measuring objects with respect to some characteristic implies that the objects differ in that characteristic; or stated in another way, that the characteristic can take on a number of different values. These properties or characteristics of an object that can assume two or more different values are referred to as a _____.
  a. Variable12
  b. -equivalence
  c. Undefined
  d. Undefined

33. _____ is the property of multiplication over addition which demonstrates that for all numbers a,b,c; a(b+c)=ab+ac, and ab+ac=a(b+c).
  a. Distributive property12
  b. -equivalence
  c. Undefined
  d. Undefined

34. The bottom part of any fraction represents the number of pieces in one whole unit. This bottom part is called the <U>denominator.</U>
  a. -equivalence
  b. Denominator12
  c. Undefined
  d. Undefined

35. The top part of the fraction is called the <U>numerator</U>. It could also be called the dividend, but _____ is preferred.
  a. Numerator12
  b. -equivalence
  c. Undefined
  d. Undefined

36. _____ (or summation) is one of the basic operations of arithmetic. In its simplest form, _____ combines two numbers, the augend and addend, into a single number, the sum.
  a. Addition12
  b. ADE classification
  c. Undefined
  d. Undefined

37. There are properties of objects that do assume one and only value, and we refer to these characteristics as _____. _____, then, are the invariables that differentiate one class of objects from another.
  a. Constants12
  b. -equivalence
  c. Undefined
  d. Undefined

38. _____ are characteristics or properties of an object that can take on one or more different values.
  a. -equivalence
  b. Variables12
  c. Undefined
  d. Undefined

Chapter 1

1. b	2. b	3. a	4. b	5. a	6. a	7. b	8. a	9. b	10. a
11. b	12. a	13. a	14. a	15. b	16. a	17. b	18. a	19. b	20. a
21. a	22. b	23. b	24. b	25. a	26. a	27. a	28. a	29. a	30. a
31. a	32. b	33. a	34. b	35. b	36. b	37. b	38. a	39. a	40. b
41. b	42. a	43. b	44. b	45. a	46. b	47. b	48. b	49. a	50. b
51. a	52. a	53. b	54. a	55. a	56. a	57. a	58. b	59. a	60. b
61. a	62. a	63. a	64. b	65. b	66. a	67. a	68. a	69. a	70. a
71. b	72. b	73. a	74. a	75. b	76. b	77. a	78. a	79. a	

Chapter 2

1. b	2. a	3. b	4. b	5. a	6. b	7. b	8. a	9. a	10. a
11. a	12. a	13. a	14. a	15. a	16. a	17. a	18. a	19. b	20. b
21. a	22. b	23. a	24. b	25. a	26. b	27. a	28. a	29. b	30. a
31. b	32. a	33. b	34. b	35. a	36. a	37. b	38. b	39. a	40. a
41. b	42. b	43. b	44. b	45. b	46. b	47. b	48. a	49. a	50. a
51. a	52. a	53. b	54. a	55. b	56. a	57. b	58. a	59. b	60. b
61. a	62. a	63. a	64. b	65. a	66. a	67. b	68. b	69. b	70. a
71. a	72. b	73. a	74. a	75. b	76. b	77. b	78. a	79. b	80. b
81. b	82. b	83. b	84. a	85. a	86. b	87. b	88. b	89. a	90. b
91. a	92. b	93. b	94. a	95. b	96. a	97. b	98. a	99. b	100. b
101. a	102. b	103. a	104. b	105. a	106. b	107. a	108. b	109. a	110. a
111. a	112. b	113. b	114. b	115. b	116. b	117. a	118. b	119. b	120. b
121. a	122. a								

Chapter 3

1. b	2. b	3. a	4. b	5. b	6. b	7. b	8. a	9. b	10. b
11. b	12. b	13. b	14. b	15. a	16. a	17. b	18. b	19. a	20. a
21. b	22. b	23. a	24. a	25. b	26. b	27. b	28. b	29. a	30. b
31. a	32. a	33. b	34. b	35. b	36. b	37. b	38. b	39. b	40. a
41. b	42. a	43. a	44. b	45. b	46. a	47. a	48. a	49. b	50. a
51. b	52. a	53. a	54. b	55. b	56. a	57. b	58. b	59. b	60. a
61. b	62. b	63. a	64. a	65. b	66. b	67. a	68. a	69. b	70. a
71. a	72. a	73. a	74. a	75. a	76. b	77. b	78. a	79. a	80. b
81. b	82. b	83. a	84. b	85. a	86. b	87. b	88. b	89. a	90. b
91. a	92. a	93. a	94. b	95. a	96. b	97. a	98. b	99. a	100. b
101. b	102. a	103. a	104. b	105. b	106. a	107. b	108. a	109. b	

ANSWER KEY

Chapter 4

1. a	2. a	3. a	4. a	5. a	6. a	7. a	8. b	9. b	10. b
11. a	12. a	13. a	14. a	15. a	16. b	17. a	18. b	19. b	20. a
21. b	22. a	23. a	24. a	25. b	26. b	27. a	28. b	29. a	30. b
31. a	32. b	33. a	34. a	35. b	36. b	37. a	38. b	39. b	40. b
41. b	42. b	43. b	44. b	45. a	46. b	47. a	48. b	49. a	50. a
51. b	52. b	53. b	54. b	55. b	56. b	57. b	58. b	59. a	60. b
61. b	62. b	63. b	64. b	65. a	66. b	67. a	68. a	69. a	70. b
71. b	72. a	73. b	74. b	75. b	76. b	77. a	78. a	79. a	80. b
81. a	82. a	83. b	84. b	85. a	86. b	87. a	88. a	89. b	90. b
91. a	92. a	93. b	94. a	95. b	96. a	97. b	98. a	99. b	100. b
101. b	102. b	103. b	104. a	105. a	106. a	107. a	108. a	109. a	110. b
111. a	112. b	113. a	114. a	115. b	116. b	117. b	118. b	119. b	120. b
121. a	122. a	123. a	124. b	125. a	126. b	127. a	128. a	129. b	

Chapter 5

1. a	2. b	3. a	4. b	5. b	6. a	7. a	8. b	9. b	10. b
11. a	12. b	13. b	14. b	15. b	16. b	17. b	18. a	19. b	20. a
21. a	22. a	23. a	24. b	25. b	26. b	27. b	28. a	29. b	30. a
31. b	32. a	33. b	34. a	35. b	36. a	37. b	38. b	39. b	40. b
41. b	42. a	43. a	44. b	45. a	46. b	47. a	48. a	49. a	50. a
51. a	52. b	53. b	54. b	55. b	56. a	57. a	58. a	59. b	60. a
61. b	62. a	63. b	64. b	65. b	66. b	67. b	68. b	69. b	70. a
71. b	72. a	73. b	74. a	75. b	76. a	77. a	78. a	79. b	80. a
81. a	82. b	83. b	84. b	85. b	86. a	87. b	88. b	89. a	90. b
91. a	92. b	93. a	94. a	95. a	96. b	97. b	98. a	99. b	100. b
101. a	102. b	103. a	104. a	105. b	106. a	107. a	108. b	109. b	110. a
111. a	112. a	113. b	114. b	115. a	116. b	117. a	118. b		

Chapter 6

1. a	2. b	3. a	4. b	5. a	6. b	7. a	8. b	9. b	10. b
11. b	12. a	13. b	14. b	15. b	16. b	17. b	18. a	19. a	20. a
21. b	22. b	23. b	24. b	25. b	26. a	27. a	28. a	29. a	30. b
31. b	32. a	33. a	34. a	35. a	36. a	37. a	38. b	39. a	40. a
41. b	42. b	43. b	44. a	45. a	46. b	47. b	48. a	49. b	50. b
51. b	52. b	53. a	54. b	55. a	56. b	57. b	58. b	59. a	60. b
61. a	62. b	63. a	64. a	65. a	66. b	67. b	68. a	69. b	70. b
71. b	72. a	73. a	74. a	75. a	76. b	77. b	78. a	79. a	80. b
81. b									

Chapter 7

1. b	2. b	3. a	4. a	5. a	6. b	7. a	8. a	9. b	10. a
11. a	12. a	13. a	14. a	15. a	16. a	17. a	18. a	19. b	20. a
21. a	22. b	23. b	24. a	25. b	26. b	27. a	28. a	29. b	30. b
31. b	32. b	33. b	34. b	35. a	36. b	37. a	38. b	39. a	40. b
41. a	42. a	43. a	44. a	45. a	46. b	47. a	48. a	49. a	50. b
51. a	52. b	53. b	54. b	55. b	56. a	57. b	58. a	59. b	60. b
61. b	62. b	63. a	64. a	65. a	66. b	67. b	68. a	69. a	70. b
71. b	72. b	73. a	74. a	75. b	76. b	77. b			

Chapter 8

1. a	2. a	3. a	4. b	5. a	6. a	7. a	8. b	9. b	10. a
11. a	12. b	13. a	14. b	15. a	16. b	17. b	18. a	19. b	20. a
21. a	22. a	23. a	24. b	25. b	26. a	27. a	28. a	29. b	30. a
31. b	32. a	33. a	34. b	35. a	36. a	37. b	38. b	39. b	40. a
41. b	42. b	43. a	44. a	45. a	46. b	47. a	48. b	49. a	50. a
51. b	52. b	53. b	54. a	55. a	56. b	57. a	58. b	59. a	60. a
61. b	62. b	63. b	64. b	65. b	66. a	67. b			

Chapter 9

1. b	2. b	3. a	4. b	5. a	6. a	7. b	8. b	9. a	10. a
11. b	12. a	13. b	14. a	15. a	16. a	17. b	18. a	19. b	20. a
21. a	22. a	23. b	24. b	25. a	26. a	27. b	28. a	29. a	30. a
31. a	32. a	33. b	34. a	35. b	36. b	37. b	38. b	39. b	40. b
41. b	42. a	43. b	44. b	45. a	46. a	47. b	48. a	49. a	50. b
51. b	52. b	53. b	54. a	55. b	56. b	57. b	58. b	59. b	60. b
61. a	62. b	63. b	64. b	65. b	66. a	67. b	68. b	69. a	70. b
71. a	72. a								

Chapter 10

1. b	2. a	3. a	4. b	5. a	6. a	7. b	8. b	9. a	10. a
11. a	12. b	13. a	14. a	15. a	16. a	17. a	18. b	19. a	20. a
21. a	22. a	23. a	24. a	25. b	26. b	27. b	28. b	29. b	30. a

Chapter 11

1. a	2. b	3. a	4. a	5. a	6. a	7. b	8. b	9. a	10. a
11. a	12. a	13. b	14. b	15. a	16. a	17. b	18. b	19. b	20. a
21. a	22. b	23. b	24. b	25. b	26. a	27. a	28. a	29. b	30. b
31. a	32. b	33. a	34. a	35. b	36. a	37. b	38. a	39. a	40. b
41. a	42. b	43. b	44. a	45. a	46. b	47. b	48. a	49. a	50. a
51. b	52. b	53. a							

ANSWER KEY

Chapter 12

1. b	2. b	3. a	4. b	5. a	6. a	7. b	8. b	9. a	10. a
11. a	12. a	13. b	14. a	15. a	16. b	17. b	18. b	19. a	20. a
21. a	22. a	23. b	24. a	25. b	26. b	27. b	28. b	29. a	30. b
31. b	32. a	33. a	34. b	35. a	36. a	37. a	38. b		

www.ingramcontent.com/pod-product-compliance
Lightning Source LLC
Chambersburg PA
CBHW082051230426
43670CB00016B/2852